THE
ANGER
WORKBOOK

an interactive guide to **anger management**

Other Books by the Authors

The Freedom From Depression Workbook
Dr. Les Carter, Dr. Frank Minirth

The Worry Workbook
Dr. Les Carter, Dr. Frank Minirth

The Choosing to Forgive Workbook
Dr. Les Carter, Dr. Frank Minirth

When Pleasing You Is Killing Me
Dr. Les Carter

The Anger Trap
Dr. Les Carter

Enough About You, Let's Talk About Me
Dr. Les Carter

Grace and Divorce
Dr. Les Carter

The Father Book
Dr. Frank Minirth, Dr. Brian Newman, Dr. Paul Warren

Imperative People
Dr. Les Carter

Love Hunger: Recovery from Food Addiction
Dr. Frank Minirth, Dr. Paul Meier, Dr. Robert Hemfelt, Dr. Sharon Sneed,
    Dr. Don Hawkins

Love Is a Choice
Dr. Robert Hemfelt, Dr. Frank Minirth, Dr. Paul Meier

Love Is a Choice Workbook
Dr. Robert Hemfelt, Dr. Frank Minirth, Dr. Paul Meier, Dr. Brian Newman,
    Dr. Deborah Newman

THE
ANGER
WORKBOOK

an interactive guide to **anger management**

Les Carter, Ph.D.
Frank Minirth, M.D.

THOMAS NELSON
Since 1798

NASHVILLE   DALLAS   MEXICO CITY   RIO DE JANEIRO

Published in Nashville, Tennessee, by Thomas Nelson. Thomas Nelson is a registered trademark of Thomas Nelson, Inc.

Scripture quotations are from the New King James Version. © 1982 by Thomas Nelson, Inc. Used by permission. All rights reserved.

Examples cited in this book are composites of the authors' actual cases in their practices. Names and facts have been changed and rearranged to maintain confidentiality.

ISBN: 978-1-4016-7543-1 (Updated edition)

The Library of Congress has catalogued the earlier edition of this guide as follows:

Library of Congress Cataloging-in-Publication Data

Carter, Les.
    The anger workbook / by Les Carter, Frank Minirth.
      p.   cm.
    ISBN-10: 0-8407-4574-5
    ISBN-13: 978-0-8407-4574-3
      1. Anger—Religious aspects—Christianity.   2. Anger—
Problems,
    exercises, etc. 3. Christian life—1960–   I. Minirth, Frank B.
    II. Meier, Paul D.   III. Title.
    BV4627.A5C38   1993
    152.4′7—dc20   92-21048
                                          CIP

Printed in the United States of America

15 16 QGF 5

Contents

Acknowledgments

The authors wish to acknowledge the help of the staff members at Thomas Nelson Publishers. They have been a joy to work with, and each one epitomizes Christian integrity in the publishing profession.

Special thanks go again to Janet Thoma for her expert guidance in this project. Few people have the clear God-given talent for written communication that she has. Also, special appreciation is expressed to Bruce Barbour for the boundless enthusiasm and expertise he lends to our work. Susan Salmon, Sue Ann Jones, and Maleah Bell are also to be commended for their fine work in the editing process.

Finally, Pam Sams deserves special acknowledgment for her tireless efforts in typing and preparing the manuscript. She is one of those invaluable behind-the-scenes workers who should receive more credit than is given.

Contents

Acknowledgments

The authors wish to acknowledge the help of the staff members at Thomas Nelson Publishers. They have been a joy to work with, and each one epitomizes Christian integrity in the publishing profession.

Special thanks go again to Janet Thoma for her expert guidance in this project. Few people have the clear God-given talent for written communication that she has. Also, special appreciation is expressed to Bruce Barbour for the boundless enthusiasm and expertise he lends to our work. Susan Salmon, Sue Ann Jones, and Maleah Bell are also to be commended for their fine work in the editing process.

Finally, Pam Sams deserves special acknowledgment for her tireless efforts in typing and preparing the manuscript. She is one of those invaluable behind-the-scenes workers who should receive more credit than is given.

Thirteen Steps Toward Anger Management

Step 1. Learn to recognize the many faces of anger.

Step 2. Admit that all angry expressions, good or bad, are the result of choices.

Step 3. Let go of excessive dependencies so your anger management is inwardly directed rather than externally determined.

Step 4. Choose to relinquish your cravings for control in exchange for freedom.

Step 5. Ground yourself in truth by setting aside idealistic myths.

Step 6. Keep your lifestyle habits consistent with your emotional composure.

Step 7. Live in humility rather than self-preoccupied pride.

Step 8. Hold your defenses to a minimum; trust your healthy assertions.

Step 9. Accept the inevitability of loneliness as you struggle to be understood.

Step 10. Relate to others as equals, neither elevating yourself above them nor accepting a position of inferiority.

Step 11. Pass along to the next generation your insights about anger.

Step 12. Avoid the temptation to rationalize your anger; assume full responsibility for who you are.

Step 13. Be accountable for your ongoing growth and open about your anger management.

Part One

Identifying
Your
Anger

1

:: What Is Anger?

■ Step 1. Learn to recognize the many faces of anger.

Tom, a slender man with a loosened tie and slightly tussled hair, sat across from Dr. Carter, explaining his reason for seeking counseling. "I don't like thinking of myself as an angry man, but I don't know any better way to describe it. I'm forty-four years old, and you would think age could mellow me, but I'm constantly frustrated and irritated.

"My wife left me two years ago because she thought I was boring. I'm an engineer, so maybe I do relate more easily to computers than to people. But honestly, I was never bad to her. I'm not argumentative and I'm always reliable in my responsibilities. She had little to worry about because I took good care of her financially and otherwise, but apparently I just wasn't good enough. I'll never understand why she couldn't love me." Tom's fists tightened as he spoke.

"What's worse, the divorce has thrown a wrench into my relationship with my two children. Gina is in her first year of college, so she's only in town during special holidays. Then her time has to be split between our two residences; plus she has several close friends in the area. I feel like I have to settle for her leftover time. Scott is a junior in high school, so he's still around. But our visits are limited mostly to weekends. And you know how a seventeen-year-old kid likes to get out. He doesn't want to just sit in Dad's dreary apartment, and I can't blame him."

As Tom spoke, Dr. Carter was absorbing more than just the facts. He was also hearing the pain in Tom's voice. Reflecting aloud, he responded, "It's very easy to convince yourself that life has dealt you an unfair blow. I'm sure you're obsessed about how you don't deserve all this. No wonder you say you're an angry man."

"That's just it, Dr. Carter. I've never really thought of myself as being angry. At least, not until now. I guess I've been surprised to know an emotion like this could get such a grip on me."

Tom should not have been so surprised. Anger is an emotion that is common to every person. Because we are imperfect people in an imperfect world, we are guaranteed to regularly encounter this emotion.

> Anger is an emotion that is common to every person. Because we are imperfect people in an imperfect world, we are guaranteed to regularly encounter this emotion.

When most people think of anger, they picture a person in a rage. They have images of slamming doors, shouting, and intimidating communication. Certainly this is part of the angry response. But anger is not that one-dimensional. It is multifaceted; therefore it should not be stereotyped. It can be found in any temperament. Whether a person is shy or extroverted, perfectionistic or laid-back, he or she can show anger in many ways. We use the term anger to describe a number of expressions: frustration, irritability, annoyance, blowing off steam, fretting. It is important to realize how each of these reactions is tied to anger.

Tom, for instance, was not a screamer; neither did he slam doors or curse when he became angry. Instead, he showed his struggle with angry emotions by withdrawing in self-pity and engaging often in critical thoughts. But Tom did not recognize these responses as expressions of anger. His former wife, on the other hand, never hid her feelings. She was capable of flying into loud, boisterous rages that rattled the windows. No one had to guess if she felt angry!

Noting this variation, Dr. Carter helped Tom see that the first step toward recovering from anger-related problems is identifying its various manifestations—recognizing its many faces.

■ ■ ■ ■

The following inventory can help you in this process too. Check the statements that apply to you.

☑ Impatience comes over me more frequently than I would like.

☐ I nurture critical thoughts quite easily.

☑ When I am displeased with someone I may shut down any communication or withdraw.

☐ I feel inwardly annoyed when family and friends do not comprehend my needs.

☐ Tension mounts within me as I tackle a demanding task.

☐ I feel frustrated when I see someone else having fewer struggles than I do.

☐ When facing an important event, I may obsessively ponder how I must manage it.

☑ Sometimes I walk in another direction to avoid seeing someone I do not like.

☐ When discussing a controversial topic, my tone of voice is likely to become persuasive.

☑ I can accept a person who admits his or her mistakes, but I have a hard time accepting someone who refuses to admit his or her own weaknesses.

☐ When I talk about my irritations I don't really want to hear an opposite point of view.

☐ I do not easily forget when someone does me wrong.

☐ When someone confronts me from a misinformed position, I am thinking of my rebuttal as he or she speaks.

☑ Sometimes my discouragement makes me want to quit.

☑ I can be quite aggressive in my business pursuits or even when playing a game just for fun.

☐ I struggle emotionally with the things in life that are not fair.

☐ Although I know it may not be right, I sometimes blame others for my problems.

☑ When someone openly speaks ill of me, my natural response is to think of how I can defend myself.

☐ Sometimes I speak slanderously about a person, not really caring how it may harm his or her reputation.

☐ I may act kindly on the outside while feeling frustrated on the inside.

☐ Sarcasm is a trait I use in expressing humor.

☑ When someone is clearly annoyed with me I too easily jump into the conflict.

☑ At times I struggle with moods of depression or discouragement.

☐ I have been known to take an "I-don't-care" attitude toward the needs of others.

☑ When I am in an authority role, I may speak too sternly or insensitively.

■ ■ ■ ■

Now go back through the inventory and count the number of statements you checked. Everyone will recognize some of these characteristics, so don't worry about marking them. If you checked ten items, your anger is probably more constant than you might like. If you checked fifteen or more, you can probably recount many disappointments and irritations. This indicates you are vulnerable to the extreme ill effects of anger, rage, and explosions of temper or to guilt, bitterness, and resentment. But don't give up! Anger can be managed if you apply an awakened mind to it.

If you are interested in gaining a broader perspective of yourself, ask a close friend or family member to complete the inventory, answering the questions as he or she thinks you would respond.

■ ■ ■ ■

You will notice from the items in the inventory that anger can be expressed by a wide array of behaviors. What expressions seem to be the most common forms of your anger? *(For instance, I turn on the silent treatment when someone bothers me; I resort to critical communication quite frequently.)*

1. I remove myself from that person and disat myself in my room not wanted to be bother

2. I curse and speak loudly

3. I just don't talk I shut people down

4. I don't let people talk over me

■ ■ ■ ■

You may show your anger in ways other than those mentioned in the inventory. It's good to discover such hidden expressions of anger; doing so implies self-awareness.

During their sessions together Tom repeatedly told Dr. Carter how he would slowly stew over daily irritants. He admitted that people, especially family members, had learned to stay out of his way when he was in one of his moods. Dr. Carter pointed out that this was a definite communication of anger that ultimately had contributed to the demise of Tom's marriage.

"Maybe I was just trying to kid myself," Tom admitted, "but I had always felt proud of being the one in our marriage who didn't have an anger problem. My wife was so vocal with her anger that I assumed my more civilized mannerisms were proof that my anger was under control."

Dr. Carter nodded. "In a sense, your anger was under control, at least to the extent that you were not a 'rageaholic.' But in another sense, it was still out of control because your personality was turning toward discouragement and your life was increasingly filled with poor relationships."

▪ DEFINING YOUR ANGER

Have you ever attempted to work on a car engine? If so, you know it can be an overwhelming task if you do not understand the engine's design and intricacies. Once you learn the function of each component, though, what at first seemed perplexing can be quite possible.

That's the way it is with anger. When we first attempt to grasp its meaning, the task of mastering it can seem impossible. But as we come to know and understand our anger, its management is far less daunting.

Let's first recognize that we live in an unjust world. A quick glance at a newspaper or the evening news will provide a sobering reminder that people can, and will, be mean-spirited and insensitive. On a broad scale we can feel frustrated by the gridlock in politics. Likewise, the increasing problem of identifying terrorists creates strain as we wonder when the next episode of evil will occur. Who would have thought a generation ago that each person entering an airport would have to remove his or her shoes in order to board a plane? Additionally, we are saddened to the point of futility by natural disasters such as tornadoes, hurricanes, earthquakes, and the like; and we have to be on guard for identity theft, computer viruses, and email scams.

Closer to home, person after person will struggle with road rage and the general futility caused by urban gridlock. Our schools have become targets for crazed shooters. We can feel perplexed by ups and downs in oil prices, while wondering if we will ever be able to sufficiently fund our retirement accounts since companies no longer provide cushy pension benefits.

Our children can no longer be allowed to roam and play outside unsupervised. Parents want to pull their hair out because Junior won't turn off the video games, and who knows what our kids are finding on the Internet that they should not be looking at. The divorce rate remains high, indicating unresolved tensions. Husbands and wives still struggle to communicate with wisdom and fairness leading the way. Single adults try to maneuver through a world that is increasingly lax regarding morality, wondering what they have to do to find meaning and happiness. And, of course, the problems created by alcohol and substance abuse have not improved over time.

It's enough to make a person feel really mad!

The net result of ongoing strains that do not recede is a feeling of insignificance. Inwardly we may ask, *Do I matter? Doesn't anyone care about my needs? Why can't I find cooperation?* Such questions then become the seed for anger.

■ ■ ■ ■

What are some of the elements of modern life in general that can keep you feeling on edge? *(For instance, I get frustrated every time I am reminded how inept governing officials seem to be; I can feel like a maniac when I am driving on the highways.)*

1. I get manic when im reminded of Hurricane Katrina

2. I get mad when A person tries to prove me wrong and embrass me

3. I get so manic on the member of my son's death.

■ ■ ■ ■

When anger surges within our personalities, it prompts a cry that insists, "Stop this madness! Quit it!" When the larger world seems uncaring or when our circle of intimates doesn't respond sympathetically, we want revenge. We want vindication. We want someone to make things right. A voice inside insists that justice must be served . . . Now!

Have you ever been pushed to the edge of your emotional limits where you wondered if anyone would ever hear you and respond appropriately to your needs? If so, you are not alone. What is more, your anger is not entirely wrong, despite what some may presume. It is right, even necessary, to seek justice. The problem with most individuals whose anger cannot be contained is not the presence of anger, but the manner in which it is handled.

■ ■ ■ ■

As you consider the many ways your anger can be aroused, what right message is beneath the emotion, even if it is not exactly managed well?

(For instance, it is reasonable for me to wish that my relatives should factor in my needs as family plans are arranged; I am not wrong for wishing that public officials should be less egotistical and more tuned into their constituents.)

1. _____

   _____

2. _____

   _____

3. _____

   _____

■ ■ ■ ■

In one of his early sessions with Dr. Carter, Tom admitted, "I'm realizing that I've experienced anger in some form my entire life. All sorts of things bug me, from news headlines to problems with coworkers to strains at home. But I must confess that I never gave two minutes of thought about its meaning until I faced the repercussions of my divorce. And frankly, I'm still not sure of the *purpose* of my anger."

> As we come to know and understand our anger, its management is far less daunting.

"Let's explore that," responded Dr. Carter. "First, notice when you do not feel angry—when you feel affirmed or understood or accepted. At those times, you feel anything but anger. Your inner self says all is well."

"You're exactly right. My anger occurs primarily when I am ignored or mistreated. So I guess you can say it is part of my defense system."

"Let's call it your emotion of self-preservation," said Dr. Carter. "Anger comes when you feel the need to clearly communicate that your personal boundaries have been violated."

Anger can be felt even when others don't see it. Anger is defined as an intent to preserve (1) personal worth, (2) essential needs, and (3) basic convictions. Let's examine each of these purposes separately.

Preserving Personal Worth

In many cases, anger is ignited when a person perceives rejection or invalidation. Whether or not that is the message intended by the speaker, the angry person feels that his or her dignity has been demeaned. Notice this common theme in the following examples:

- A wife tries to tell her husband she does not have the time or energy to run errands for him as he has requested. Besides, she believes, he is just being lazy; he could run the errands himself. So she tells him his request may not receive the high priority he wants. He responds by reminding her of the hard work he does so the bills can be paid. When he accuses her of being selfish she becomes angry, feeling frustrated because he will not acknowledge her contributions to the family.

- A computer salesman is doing well in his work, performing beyond his quota. Then the boss decides to give part of the salesman's territory to a less experienced worker, forcing the successful salesman to forfeit new leads. He feels unfairly treated, but when he tries to talk to his boss about this problem the boss says his feelings are out of line. The salesman feels his value to the company is grossly underestimated.

- A father who overhears his two teenage sons disagreeing about something scolds them harshly for arguing. When one of the brothers tries to talk calmly to his father, he is reprimanded even more severely. The boys retreat to their bedroom, grumbling about Dad's constant condescension.

Each of these examples differs greatly in its anger-producing circumstances. Yet there is a common thread: the lack of respect felt by the wife, the salesman, and the teenagers. Whether or not it was the intention of the sender, the message they perceived was, *Your worth is none of my concern.* In personal communications, perceptions are more powerful than intentions.

■ ■ ■ ■

Have you ever struggled with a feeling of being devalued by others? List some recent examples of times when your worth was not acknowledged. *(For instance, my spouse tunes me out when I have something important to say; I work harder than anyone at my job, but I haven't gotten a raise in more than a year.)*

1. I WORK really harde and never be acknowledge
2. When people stste I come of wich a strong Atthide
3. When my boyfriend lieds to me When he knows he been cheating
4. When I'm rejectec or Judge becsuse of my PAss...

Adults can be ultrasensitive because of childhood experiences that left them feeling unworthy. How about you? What were your parents like when you were a child? How was your worth (or the lack of it) communicated? *(For instance, my dad often told me what was wrong with my work but not what was good about it.)*

1. my mother wk alot so my sistur was liked my mom but I wantec my
2. When my childen quts me at me like its my fault
3. beening rejected

■ ■ ■ ■

Christianity offers great hope to those whose worth is not acknowledged by their fellow human beings. We are taught that God places high value on each person who calls on Him. Even when we fail to live perfectly, that worth is not erased.

■ ■ ■ ■ ▫

Despite all his riches, King David struggled with the idea that he might be of real value to his Creator. He wrote, "What is man that You are mindful of him, and the son of man that You visit him?" (Psalm 8:4). Yet the Lord assured David he had been created with glory and majesty. What does this mean to you?

_____

_____

Consider Jesus' parable in Matthew 13:45–46: "Again, the kingdom of heaven is like a merchant seeking beautiful pearls, who, when he had found one pearl of great price, went and sold all that he had and bought it." This brief parable can be understood as depicting God's willingness to give all that He has for one single soul. How does this apply to you?

_____

_____

■ ■ ■ ■ ▫

Tom carefully considered how these ideas applied to his anger. "You're telling me I was angry because I felt my wife was not acknowledging my worth. That makes sense because I felt unappreciated much of the time," he said.

"I am also saying your anger was exaggerated because you were so sharply focused on her messages of invalidation that you forgot about your inherent worth offered by God Himself."

"I've got to tell you," Tom said, "that I have heard the concept of my God-given worth described many times, but it hasn't had much impact on my ability to manage my emotions."

That's the case for many of us. It is not enough to merely intellectualize our God-given worth. We need to choose to accept our worth, even when another human chooses not to. This choice can have a major effect on the intensity of our angry emotions. It does not mean we will stop experiencing anger, but we will be less affected by others.

For example, Tom learned to moderate his anger by reminding himself that when his former wife rejected him she was not necessarily correct in her evaluation of him. So, rather than wishing he could convince her of his worth (an effort that perpetuated his anger), he could cling instead to his value before God.

■ ■ ■ ■

How about you? Who in your life have you allowed to "play God" and make you vulnerable to ongoing anger? *(For instance, my sister persistently criticizes my child-rearing methods, making me doubt my abilities as a parent.)*

1. _____

_____

2. _____

_____

3. _____

_____

4. _____

_____

■ ■ ■ ■

Preserving Essential Needs

In the animal kingdom, survival is the name of the game. An animal, be it a bird, beast, or fish, is constantly looking for the simplest ingredients to provide life for another day. Little else is of true importance.

Humans also have basic survival needs, but ours are much more complex. The Bible recognizes this fact in its many "one another" passages. For example, we are told to love one another, to bear one another's burdens, to encourage one another, to confess to one another, and to respect one another. These (and many more) instructions highlight our intricate system of needs that must be satisfactorily addressed if we are to have emotional well-being. When our essential needs are not addressed, or when they are invalidated, the result is emotional turmoil. We feel hurt and angry.

■ ■ ■ ▪

While it is impossible to list all of your needs, what are some of the major personal needs in your life? *(For example, I need social activity, time alone, assistance from a coworker.)*

1. _____

_____

2. _____

_____

3. _____

_____

4. _____

_____

5. _____

_____

■ ■ ■ ▪

If you compare your list of major needs with someone else's, you will probably find some distinct differences. For example, a person with a busy schedule may feel a strong need for promptness in family members and coworkers, while a more laid-back person may cite a greater need for stimulating work. This is to be expected. Each of us has a different temperament, causing us to interact with differing motives and desires. Also, no two people have the same background or experiences, so each of us enters adulthood with unique issues of importance.

■ ■ ■ ▪

Can you think of some recent examples of needs that have been unmet or improperly addressed in your life? *(For instance, my husband does not share my need for regular communication about personal matters.)*

1. _____

_____

2. _____

_____

3. _____

_____

4. _____

_____

How do these unmet needs feed your anger? That is, how do they in-fluence your emotional well-being? *(For instance, I need my children to cooperate in helping with household chores, and when they fail to realize this I become grouchy.)*

_____

_____

_____

_____

■ ■ ■ ■

The angry person demonstrates a weariness of having to live without his or her basic needs being noticed by others. The resulting anger is a type of protest: *Can't anyone understand who I am? I've got legitimate is-sues that you should care about!* In many cases, the anger is unquestion-ably legitimate because it is normal to expect some of these needs to be met. In other instances, however, the anger can be misguided or over-stated because it represents a picky or selfish demand (such as a teen-ager who is angry because he or she "needs" an expensive item of fad clothing).

Notice in the following examples how unmet needs feed anger:

  A wife is regularly upset with her husband, quick to criticize and fretful over minor matters. Even when the husband attempts to please her she remains disgruntled because she is sure his im-perfections will resurface later on. She has convinced herself she needs perfection in her home, and because this is impossible she stays chronically angry.

- A teenager grimaces as he watches his buddies enjoy greater social freedoms than he has. He feels hampered in developing the social ties necessary to his developmental needs. He eventually responds with a rebelliousness that causes his parents to become even more dictatorial.

- A single woman takes her car to a mechanic who tells her she needs major repairs. She lets him do the work but feels annoyed because she is not certain he is being truthful; she also is worried about the added burden to her budget.

In each of these examples a need was unmet, creating an atmosphere that was ripe for anger. The wife's anger was propelled by her need for perfect order. The teenager was inhibited in his need for meaningful social interaction. The single woman's anger was fed by her need for a more trustworthy laborer and for greater financial freedom. Through anger they were expressing a wish for self-preservation; they were hopeful someone would satisfy their needs.

> And my God shall supply all your need according to His riches in glory by Christ Jesus.
> —Philippians 4:19

Philippians 4:19 tells us, "And my God shall supply all your need according to His riches in glory by Christ Jesus." The implication is that we need not fret when humans refuse to acknowledge our needs. This does not mean we never try to communicate our legitimate needs; instead, we ultimately choose to recognize that life can and will go on, even when we feel inhibited by insensitive humans.

Tom seemed particularly ready to grasp this truth. "The idea of anger being related to needs strikes close to home. For the past two years my needs have been put on the back burner. I really need a sense of family, but I can't get satisfaction because my family has gone off in several directions. The same goes for my friends. When you get divorced, your former relationships are never the same," he said.

"In your anger," Dr. Carter told him, "you are harboring hope that those needs will someday be restored. The uncertainty that those needs will be met makes you more vulnerable to emotional highs and lows."

Tom decided that while some of his anger was legitimate, and therefore expected, he would also learn to focus on the larger truth that God would not let him get so far down on his luck that he had no hope. "I have to remind myself every day that not all my needs have been neglected. I still have food in my stomach and a roof over my head. I have friends who will listen when I call. I have a decent job. Sometimes it's easy to act like nobody cares about my needs, but that really isn't true."

■ ■ ▪ ▪

Respond to the following thoughts:

When someone ignores my legitimate needs I can avoid responding with anger by _____

_____

I know I am too worried about my needs when I _____

_____

■ ■ ▪ ▪

Preserving Basic Convictions

Nancy, a middle-aged housewife involved in many community activities, told Dr. Minirth, "Many times I feel irritated about matters that have nothing to do with me. For example, I get mad when I see how the entertainment industry portrays sex and violence to our young people. And it just burns me up when the media fawn all over these celebrities as if they are gods and goddesses. Can't they understand the role they are playing in the deterioration of our society's moral fiber?"

Dr. Minirth nodded sympathetically as he listened. "I'm in full agreement with you. We really are witnessing an erosion of morals, and much of it is encouraged by people who only care about making money for their own selfish pursuits. It's hard not to feel angry about these things."

Nancy responded, "But Dr. Minirth, I seem to be more troubled about this type of problem than others are. I mean, you just said you agree with my viewpoint, but I doubt that you feel as tense as I do about it most of the time."

"There's a fine line, Nancy, between knowing when to stand firmly for your convictions and when to accept the imperfections you see in your world. Without question, I agree there are times we need to take unwavering stands for our convictions. Sometimes we do this publicly, sometimes just in our most cherished relationships. When anger is so much a part of your personality that you lose your capacity to find peace, it's an indication your good beliefs are, ironically, working against you."

As Nancy's example illustrates, we sometimes feel angry when we realize others are insensitive to our most fundamental convictions. Mature adults definitely need to have a firm foundation of beliefs to guide their lives, yet we also need to know how to remain composed when others do not share the same beliefs.

Notice in the following examples how firm convictions can be a springboard for anger:

- A laborer prides himself on his commonsense approach to his work. His supervisor, however, is sloppy in attending to the details that would make projects go smoothly. The laborer is a chronic grumbler who gladly expresses his dissatisfaction to anyone who wants to discuss the management's inept habits.

- A shopper in the checkout line at the grocery store witnesses a mother fussing rudely with her four-year-old son. This shopper becomes so flustered by the mother's behavior she leaves her keys on the cashier's counter, then spends twenty minutes trying to remember where she put them.

- A college student watching the evening news is increasingly incensed as a politician expresses views contrary to her own. She becomes a regular participant in public demonstrations that frequently become belligerent and bitter.

- A dad learns that his son has been hibernating in his bedroom for hours playing video games. He seeks out his wife to gripe about the lack of discipline in their home, and how it is her fault.

In each of these examples, the person was angry because his or her fundamental conviction was ignored by others. Ironically, the conviction itself may have been understandable, but the emotional result was dissatisfactory.

■ ■ ■ ▪

List below some of the convictions you cling to that can result in feelings of anger. *(For instance, I believe smokers should refrain from smoking in public places.)*

1. _____

_____

2. _____

_____

3. _____

_____

4. _____

_____

■ ■ ■ ▪

It is difficult to know how to manage feelings of anger when our convictions are violated. Many of us who were trained to think in black-and-white terms hold so firmly to our beliefs that rigid dogmatism sets in. The more dogmatic we become the more easily angered we are. This can be a case of having too much of a good thing.

In the apostle Paul's first letter to the Corinthians, he addressed several subjects that had caused angry disputes among church members. In chapter 8 of this letter, as he was focusing on the topic of eating meat previously offered to idols, he cut to the heart of their anger when he warned the Corinthians that knowledge could make them arrogant. "Knowledge puffs up," he said (v. 1). It is possible, he explained, to be so filled with good opinions that those opinions seem to give too much justification for unloving outbursts. In other words, being right can lead to being wrong.

■ ■ ■ ■

Can you think of situations when your anger is created by a conviction that is too strongly held? *(For instance, when I learn that a person has anxiety problems I become judgmental; I go into a rage when my spouse spends more money than we have budgeted.)*

1. _____

_____

2. _____

_____

IS ANGER GOOD OR BAD?

By defining anger as the emotion of self-preservation of your worth, needs, and convictions, it is easier to detect your moments of vulnerability to it. But while we recognize our times of vulnerability, we still need to answer a common question: Is anger good or bad?

The answer is, it all depends. There are times when anger is incorrectly associated with trivial matters. And there are times when it may be associated with legitimate concerns, but is managed irresponsibly. Balance is found when anger is linked to a reasonable issue and is communicated in a proper manner. This requires delicate sifting through the options of anger management, a challenge to be explored in the next chapter.

2

:: Managing Your Anger

■ **Step 2. Admit that all angry expressions, good or bad, are the result of choices.**

Nancy, the woman described in Chapter 1 who talked with Dr. Minirth about her dogmatic convictions, told him, "In the past I was trained to think anger was totally bad. Now I'm realizing there are moments when it has its place, but I'm still learning to keep my anger from crossing the line into an inappropriate expression."

"Out of curiosity," asked Dr. Minirth, "how did you learn that anger is bad?"

"When I was a girl, my father had a tendency to explode in rages. Sometimes he was easy to relate to, but then a dark mood could envelop him and he could go into tirades over minor problems. My mother and I were afraid of him. I vowed I would never feel anger like that."

"Understandably, you recognized, even at an early age, that a rageful anger has no place in a healthy personality," Dr. Minirth reflected. "But I'm hearing you imply you went too far in your good intentions. You learned to hide your anger because you believed it was always wrong."

"I really did believe that," Nancy replied. "I know now that anger can have some positive functions. But it's not easy erasing those old impressions from my mind."

Is Nancy alone in her confusion? Not at all. Virtually all of us have witnessed in others and/or felt in ourselves the strong, harmful type of anger. It is painful. It destroys. So it is easy to conclude, *If this is what anger leads to, I want nothing to do with it.*

■ ■ ■ ■

How about you? What types of harmful anger have you been exposed to? *(For instance, my brother used to speak awful insults when he became angry.)*

1. _____

_____

2. _____

_____

3. _____

_____

■ ■ ■ ■

Once you have learned to identify anger and understand its meaning, you can then learn to distinguish right and wrong ways of managing it. Although you may not always like the presence of your anger, you can make choices about how you handle it.

> **Although you may not always like the presence of your anger, you can make choices about how you handle it.**

This concept of choices excited Nancy. "Maybe I've been dense regarding emotional matters, but I never really thought about choices before. I've always just assumed that anger would go away as soon as my circumstances took a turn for the better. Acknowledging my choices puts the responsibility for my emotions squarely on my own shoulders. That means I don't have to be a prisoner to unwanted events."

Dr. Minirth continued with Nancy's insight. "By making anger management a matter of choice, you are saying, 'Although my world may not be stable, I can be stable in it.' You are utilizing real spiritual strength."

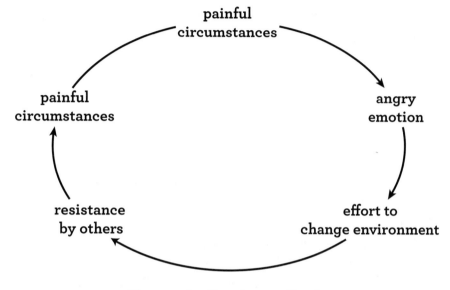

Nonproductive Anger Cycle

The diagram illustrates how people keep themselves in a nonproductive anger cycle. First there is a painful circumstance in the form of (1) a message of devaluation, (2) an unmet need, or (3) an event counter to convictions. This painful circumstance triggers the angry emotion.

At this point, most people will respond to their anger by attempting to change the environment (for example, convincing others of their errors, moving to a different part of the house, or plunging into a project to let off some steam). This is not always wrong, but it can be risky because it does not guarantee anger relief. Instead, it can lead to increased friction in personal relationships, which increases the angry person's emotional confusion. The net result is that the original angry emotion is not adequately resolved, leaving the individual vulnerable to an unhealthy build-up of tension.

By choosing to manage your anger, though, you can break this endless cycle. Sometimes you may, indeed, determine that changing your environment will be helpful. But other times you may decide that emotional stability will have to come from internally sifting through your emotional options.

■ ■ ■ ■

When you consider the idea of choices in anger, do you feel increased frustration or increased hope? Explain.

_____

_____

_____

FIVE WAYS TO HANDLE ANGER

No two people are exactly alike in managing anger. Temperaments and circumstances differ widely. But we can identify five general choices that can be made when anger arises: (1) suppression, (2) open aggression, (3) passive aggression, (4) assertiveness, or (5) dropping it. The first three choices tend to perpetuate anger. The last two can lead to success. Let's examine each separately.

Suppressing Anger

Many people hesitate to admit their own anger. Like Nancy, they usually have witnessed some ill effects of this emotion, so they resolve not to be lowered to expressions that seem overbearing or crude. Some are perfectionists who never want to appear rattled or weak, so they stubbornly maintain a veneer of existing above problems associated with anger. Others have such a deep history of poor conflict resolution that they assume that exposing their frustration will create more problems than it will solve. Either way, when an anger-producing circumstance occurs, these people stoically put on a good front and pretend to feel no tension at all. They express mild surprise that anyone would assume they might be angry. "Who me? Angry? No, really, everything is just fine."

As Nancy spoke with Dr. Minirth she admitted that suppressing anger seemed like her only plausible choice. "I knew I could not afford to rage like my father did. Besides, that's just not me. It would ruin my reputation, and I can't imagine where I would be if I lost my social standing."

Dr. Minirth replied, "So expressing anger means you would lose your ability to make friends?"

"Well, yes!" she said with amazement in her voice. "I mean, how can you possibly keep good relations if you are known for being angry? You would have no friends at all."

Nancy was thinking in an all-or-nothing pattern that is common to those who persistently suppress anger. *Because all anger is bad,* this thinking goes, *I can never afford to express it.*

■ ■ ■ ■

How about you? Do you ever hold your anger inside in an unhealthy way? You may not be as black and white in your thinking as Nancy was. But you could be prone to this habit in your own way. Check the items that apply to you to determine how likely you are to suppress your anger.

- ☐ I am very image conscious. I don't like to let others know my problems.

- ☐ Even when I feel very flustered I portray myself publicly as having it all together.

- ☐ I am rather reserved about sharing my problems or frustrations.

- ☐ If a family member or friend upsets me I can let days pass without even mentioning it.

- ☐ I have a tendency to be depressed and moody.

- ☐ Resentful thinking is common for me, although many people would never suspect it.

- ☐ I have suffered with physical complaints (for example, headaches, stomach ailments, sleep irregularity).

- ☐ There are times when I wonder if my opinions or preferences are really valid.

☐ Sometimes I feel paralyzed when confronted by an unwanted situation.

☐ I'm not inclined to initiate conversations about sensitive or troublesome topics.

■ ■ ■ ■

If you checked five or more of these statements you probably have a well-established pattern of repressing your anger. This represents a type of emotional dishonesty in your relationships.

Why do people habitually suppress their anger?

As in Nancy's case, many people learn to suppress their anger because of fears caused by authority figures who have invalidated their anger. Whereas anger is common to all people, these people have been trained to think that their anger is *not* normal. They have a history of being invalidated when their perceptions differ from others'. They fear powerful retaliation if they register disagreement or even if they only demonstrate uniqueness. And they are so convinced their expressions will come to no good end they succumb to a "what's-the-use?" mentality. Their suppression of anger represents a feeling of personal defeat.

■ ■ ■ ■

When are you most inclined to suppress your expressions of anger? *(For instance, my husband doesn't respect my opinions, so I have learned never to argue with him about major subjects.)*

1. _____

_____

2. _____

_____

3. _____

_____

■ ■ ■ ■

Another explanation for suppressing anger is a mind-set of moral superiority. Some people assume that only "heathens" become angry, and they are determined to rise above this kind of "riffraff" behavior.

Usually these people have a long-standing tendency toward rigidness. Being very image conscious, they have self-imposed a list of standards they must constantly follow. Often these standards are religiously based. Other times they are part of an overall need for approval from respectable people. In either case, these people assume it is dangerous to expose any elements of their imperfect humanness that might reduce their lofty position above others.

■ ■ ■ ■

What attitudes do you hold that might cause you to suppress your emotions so you can maintain a position of superiority? *(For instance, I can never let my children know when I am feeling upset; I've got to keep a flawless reputation at work.)*

1. _____

   _____

2. _____

   _____

3. _____

   _____

■ ■ ■ ■

Most counselors agree that suppressing anger ultimately does nothing to eliminate it. Suppressed anger resembles moss living in the damp, dark corner of a basement. You may not see it, but it is spreading. It does not go away on its own. So, even though suppression is a choice, let's agree that it is not a desirable one.

Open Aggression

When most people think of anger, they imagine open aggression, a self-preserving stand for personal worth, needs, and convictions *at someone else's expense*. This is the category of anger that includes explosiveness, rage, intimidation, and blame. But it is not limited to these extreme forms of expression. It can also include bickering, criticism, griping, and sarcasm. Open aggression arises from a focus that so strongly emphasizes personal needs there is a powerful insensitivity to the needs of others. Foul play, therefore, is virtually guaranteed.

Tom, the divorced man who spoke with Dr. Carter about his increasing bitterness, admitted, "I used to think of myself as mild mannered. But when it became apparent that my wife was serious about leaving, my anger started getting out of hand."

> Open aggression arises from a focus that so strongly emphasizes personal needs there is a powerful insensitivity to the needs of others.

"Perhaps you had some legitimate things to say," Dr. Carter suggested, "but they came out in unruly ways."

"They sure did. It was as though an internal monster had control of me. I was capable of saying very hurtful things. And I'm ashamed to admit that I would sometimes speak in very critical ways. Even now, after two years, I'm still capable of snapping at people or speaking impatiently. I really have to be on my guard."

Dr. Carter told Tom, "I wish I could tell you it is rare for a person to use this aggressive form of anger. But if my experience with people holds true, it's very common, even for decent people, to lose control and let their anger fly."

Openly aggressive anger can be easily identified because it does not hide in the same fashion as suppressed anger.

■ ■ ■ ■

Check the items that apply to you to assess your inclination toward this pattern.

☐ I can be blunt and forceful when someone does something to frustrate me.

☐ As I speak my convictions my voice becomes increasingly louder.

☐ When someone confronts me about a problem, I am likely to offer a ready rebuttal.

☐ No one has to guess my opinion; I'm known for having unwavering viewpoints.

☐ When something goes wrong, I focus so sharply on fixing the problem that I overlook others' feelings.

☐ I have a history of getting caught in bickering matches with family members.

☐ During verbal disagreements with someone, I tend to repeat myself several times.

☐ I find it hard to keep my thoughts to myself when it is obvious that someone else is wrong.

☐ I have a reputation for being strong willed.

☐ I tend to give advice, even when others have not asked for it.

■ ■ ■ ■

If you checked five or more of these statements, you probably have a pattern of open aggressive anger. Predictably, you will have ongoing struggles with relatives and close associates. Two major explanations can be given for open aggression: (1) emotional energy is expended on nonessentials, and (2) deep insecurity causes increased efforts to be heard. Let's look more closely at these two ideas.

First, much anger is related to trivial imperfections that simply won't go away. Each of us knows that problems will always be a part of our sinful, imperfect world. And we also admit that differentness will be part of every relationship, sometimes with frustrating results. But do we accept these facts emotionally in a way that keeps us composed?

Life's imperfections guarantee that we will have many "loose ends" in our relationships. Examples of these imperfections abound:

A parent of an adult child makes a nuisance of himself or herself by horning in on the adult child's lifestyle.

A child leaves clothes on the bedroom floor, even though the parent has insisted a hundred times that the room should be kept neat.

- No matter how clearly you express your needs to your mate, you just don't feel understood.
- A coworker handles a job in his or her unique way, believing that way is better than yours.
- A friend is chronically late to social engagements.
- Plans for family time fall apart because of family members' conflicting schedules.

The list of imperfections is endless, but emotionally balanced people accept these imperfections and acknowledge their limits to force people into a mold. They learn to live with some problems rather than attempting to erase them all. But the aggressive person simply will not rest until these problems are solved once and for all. (Back to the all-or-nothing thinking again.) The result, of course, is ever-increasing tension.

■ ■ ■ ■

How about you? What imperfections do you have a hard time accepting?

1. _____

_____

2. _____

_____

3. _____

_____

4. _____

_____

■ ■ ■ ■

The second major reason for aggressive anger is personal insecurity. In the most positive light, an angry person wishes to communicate, *Hey, notice that I have legitimate needs. Respect me!* Not only is this a normal thought, it can actually be healthy to think this way.

But aggressive persons take this normal desire too far. They are so needy and desirous of respect they communicate in unbending demands:

You have to acknowledge me. I can't stand it when I am not affirmed. I'll fall apart if you disregard me. Their emotional stability hangs by a thread, dependent upon others' cooperation. (We will explore the link between anger and dependency more thoroughly in Chapter 3.)

How about you? When does insecurity cause you to become openly angry? *(For instance, I snap at my wife if she disagrees with my point of view.)*

1. _____

_____

2. _____

_____

3. _____

_____

As in the case of suppressed anger, let's acknowledge that open aggression is an option for expressing anger, albeit a poor one. No doubt, you can recall that when this form of anger is used it virtually always escalates interpersonal strains. You can continue in this mode, but be ready for recurring power plays in your relationships. Remember, it is a choice.

Passive Aggression

Some people are determined not to succumb to the temptation to be rageful in their anger. Rightly recognizing that open aggression creates an atmosphere of great disrespect, they refuse to explode loudly or get caught in games of verbal abuse. That's the good news. The bad news, however, is that these individuals can still communicate their anger destructively, but in a veiled manner. By doing so, they become susceptible to passive aggression. Many of these people already have a habit of suppressing anger, but they are incapable of holding it inside permanently.

Like open aggression, anger expressed through passive aggression involves preserving personal worth, needs, and convictions at someone else's expense. But it differs in that it is accomplished in a quieter manner, causing less personal vulnerability.

■ ■ ■ ■

The following checklist provides some examples of passive aggressive anger. Check the items that apply to you.

- ☐ When I am frustrated, I become silent, knowing it bothers other people.

- ☐ I am prone to sulk and pout.

- ☐ When I don't want to do a project, I will procrastinate. I can be lazy.

- ☐ When someone asks if I am frustrated, I will lie and say, "No, everything is fine."

- ☐ There are times when I am deliberately evasive so others won't bother me.

- ☐ I sometimes approach work projects halfheartedly.

- ☐ When someone talks to me about my problems, I stare straight ahead, deliberately obstinate.

- ☐ I complain about people behind their backs but resist the opportunity to be open with them face to face.

- ☐ Sometimes I become involved in behind-the-scenes misbehavior.

- ☐ I sometimes refuse to do someone a favor, knowing this will irritate him or her.

■ ■ ■ ■

If you checked five or more items, you show a strong inclination toward using passive aggression to express your anger. You may think you are succeeding in putting limits on your anger, but you are only communicating the anger in a way that will cause future tensions.

Passive aggression is caused by a need to have control with the least amount of vulnerability. This form of anger is different from suppression in that the person knows he or she is angry (in contrast to suppressed anger, which is denied). But because this person assumes it is too risky to be open, he or she frustrates others by subtle sabotage.

The need for control is evidence of a strong competitive spirit. Whereas healthy relationships do not keep score regarding right and wrong, the passive aggressive person is out to win. Like the openly aggressive person, the passive aggressive person is engaged in a battle for superiority. But this person has cleverly realized that too much honesty about personal differences lessens his or her ability to maintain an upper hand. In contrast, sly forms of handling anger tend to keep him or her in the driver's seat.

■ ■ ■ ■

Assuming for a moment that superiority over others is a worthy goal, what "advantages" might you find in the use of passive aggression? *(For instance, others will become increasingly flustered, causing me to seem much more composed.)*

1. _____

_____

2. _____

_____

3. _____

_____

Of course, for each apparent advantage there are many long-term disadvantages. Can you think of some? *(For instance, grudges become more fixed in my relationships.)*

1. _____

_____

2. _____

_____

3. _____

_____

■ ■ ■ ■

As we did in describing suppression and open aggression, let's acknowledge that passive aggression is indeed a choice for expressing anger. But it, too, perpetuates unwanted tension.

Assertive Anger

If anger is defined as preserving personal worth, needs, and convictions, then assertive anger means this preservation is accomplished while considering the needs and feelings of others. When you communicate with true assertion, you combine firmness with respectfulness. This form of anger can actually help relationships to grow. It represents a mark of personal maturity and stability.

In years past, the word *assertive* has been used extensively by persons who advocate very forthright positions. As a result, many people came to think of the term as meaning pushy or abrasive.

■ ■ ■ ■

What about you? Can you think of an example of presumed assertiveness that was in reality a turnoff? *(For instance, a workplace manager who "assertively" reprimanded a coworker for being late, but the reprimand resulted in a longstanding feud between the two.)*

_____

_____

■ ■ ■ ■

True assertiveness is not abrasive, nor is it meant to harm. Ephesians 4:26 gives a green light to assertiveness by telling us, "Be angry, and do not sin." This means there can be times when it is healthy to address concerns about personal

> Be angry, and do not sin.—Ephesians 4:26

worth, needs, and convictions, but it should be done in a manner that keeps the door open for ongoing love.

Notice the following examples of assertive expressions of anger:

- An overworked church member can politely but firmly say no to a request to do even more projects.

- A parent can state guidelines for discipline without resorting to debate or condescension toward the child.

- When swamped by more responsibilities than he or she can manage, a person can request help from friends.

- A tired mom can tell her family she will take a thirty-minute break with no interruptions.

- Spouses can talk about their differences, offering helpful suggestions without raising their voice or repeating their messages incessantly.

- A family member may choose to pursue an independent activity instead of succumbing to the persistent demands of extended family.

Dr. Minirth talked with Nancy about the possibility of channeling her anger into the assertive style. "There are times when it is normal to take a stand in your relationships. Your struggle with anger tells me you may, indeed, have some legitimate needs that have been unheeded. Your goal will be to communicate your emotions in a constructive fashion."

"I'm really having to adjust my thinking about anger," Nancy reflected. "It will be new for me to think of it as something that might be constructive."

"Think of it this way," Dr. Minirth encouraged. "If you feel disrespected or ignored and you do nothing to properly address your needs, eventually you will become sour and your contributions to relationships will be negative. Assertiveness allows you to keep a clean slate with others."

Two key reminders will help you learn to communicate assertively: (1) Make sure the issues receiving your attention are not trivial. Instead, expend your emotional energy on subjects that matter. For example, it is trivial for spouses to argue about the color of socks the husband wears, but it is legitimate to address annoying social habits. (2) Be aware that your tone of voice can help create an atmosphere of respect for others. This is consistent with the Ephesians 4:15 instruction to speak the truth in love.

■ ■ ■ ■

As you survey your current relationships, what are some legitimate needs you might openly address? *(For instance, my brother ignores me when I ask him to help with our elderly parents' household chores.)*

1. _____

_____

2. _____

_____

3. _____

_____

4. _____

_____

As you communicate your needs and convictions, what will you need to do to ensure that your behavior is assertive rather than aggressive? *(For instance, when I talk to my brother about helping with our parents' chores, I'll explain my preferences without heaping guilt on him.)*

1. _____

_____

2. _____

_____

3. _____

_____

4. _____

_____

■ ■ ■ ■

Assertiveness is not always easy. It requires self-discipline and respect for the dignity of others. It implies that we are not just pushing selfish agendas on them. And it requires us to put our communications into the context of the "big picture," anticipating how it will affect future interactions. Therefore, caution is needed as assertiveness is used. James 1:19 puts it this way: "Let every man be swift to hear, slow to speak, slow to wrath."

■ ■ ■ ■

Respond to the following sentences:

When I speak assertively, I still want others to know _____

_____

Although I want to be taken seriously by others, I want my reputation

to be _____

_____

■ ■ ■ ■

Dropping Anger

Of the choices involving anger the most difficult one is to let it go. There are times when you can have appropriate convictions to communicate, yet assertiveness does not produce the desired results. Or it could be you have succeeded in making as many adjustments as possible in your world, yet imperfections continue to haunt you. At this point one of your options is to choose to drop your anger.

Dropping your anger means you accept your inability to completely control circumstances and you recognize your personal limits. This option includes tolerance of differences as well as choosing to forgive. Notice how anger is dropped in the following examples:

- A wife recognizes that, despite her discussions with her husband, he will always be perfectionistic. As a result, she draws her boundaries so she will not always have to comply with his finicky preferences, but she also learns to accept him as he is.

- An adult son admits that his father has chosen not to love him. So, rather than carry a grudge, he decides to forgive his father while also charting a new style of fathering with his own children.

- A husband comes to terms with the truth that his wife is not as organized as he would like, so he chooses not to criticize her shortcomings.

- Rather than griping about company policy, an employee decides that no job is perfect, so he will do his best work in spite of his differences in preference.

■ ■ ■ ■

What about you? What are some situations in your life in which you could drop your anger?

1. _____

_____

2. _____

_____

3. _____

_____

4. _____

_____

■ ■ ■ ■

When Tom, still bitter about his divorce, talked with Dr. Carter about dropping his anger toward his former wife, he confessed, "What makes this choice so difficult is the fact that she never gave me a chance. In all our years together she felt angry, but I don't think she was committed to constructively discussing our issues. My problem was that I responded to her anger poorly instead of using constructive assertiveness. That only made matters worse."

"So, knowing that you are having to live with the consequences of divorce unnecessarily, it is hard to forgive her and move on," Dr. Carter summarized.

"That's an understatement!" said Tom. "I know I need to accept her rejection and move on, but it's not going to feel natural. I'm the kind of person who likes to tie up all the loose ends."

For Tom and others like him, dropping the anger means accepting the fact that anger management does not hinge on someone else's decisions. While a spirit of teamwork can be most beneficial to anger reduction, it is not a must. Ephesians 4:31 tells us that such problems as bitterness, anger, and malice can be "put away." Then Ephesians 4:32 instructs us to choose kindness and forgiveness as a way of life.

■ ■ ■ ■

Think carefully and respond to the following statements:

Letting go of my anger is difficult because _____

_____

I realize life isn't always fair, so I need to accept _____

_____

■ ■ ■ ■

Let's keep in mind that choosing to drop your anger is far different from suppressing it. Suppression represents phoniness while dropping anger represents a commitment to godliness. The person who chooses to let go of the anger is fully aware that grudges are an option, but he or she chooses instead to opt for a cleaner life anchored in kindness.

One warning: A common problem that often arises when people attempt to drop their anger is that sometimes the anger returns at a later date. For example, a woman who chooses to forgive her rebellious adult son may live in peace until she learns new information about his misdeeds. Then old frustrations again well up in anger. Does this mean she was unsuccessful in her earlier decision to set aside her anger? Not at all. When we decide to let go of anger, there may be moments when we need to remind ourselves of our original decision to drop it, and we may need to "sign up" once again. Only God is capable of removing memories "as far as the east is from the west" (Psalm 103:12).

The following are some suggestions to help you when you choose to drop your anger:

■ Make yourself accountable to a trusted friend. Let that person know when you are struggling.

- Admit that you are not exactly perfect, which means you should be willing to extend the same grace that you want to receive.

- Choose to live in kindness and forgiveness only today. You don't have the ability to decide what your emotions will be for the many years ahead.

- Write out your feelings. Then read over them with the attitude that you will turn them loose.

■ ■ ■ ■

Respond to the following statement:

The thing that would help me most in dropping my anger would be *(for instance, accepting the truth that others will be imperfect)*

_____

■ LOOKING AHEAD

Nancy and Tom each benefited greatly by taking responsibility for their own emotional expressions. Both had been prisoners of their own anger, because they had never learned to understand its meaning and never realized the choices that could be made when it appeared. You, too, will find that, when your emotions become less mysterious and more familiar to you, they will stop controlling you.

Often, people have trouble making good choices for handling their anger because they have not resolved the tensions linked to their environments. While this is sometimes due to current unmet needs, it can also involve unmet needs in the past, as well. We will explore some of these major environmental barriers to successful anger management in the next four chapters.

Part Two

Anger
Thrives on
Unmet Needs

3

:: Why Can't You Just Love Me?

■ Step 3. Let go of excessive dependencies so your anger management is inwardly directed rather than externally determined.

Anger does not arise in a vacuum. As mentioned in Chapter 1, each of us has basic psychological needs that have to be adequately met if we are to enjoy emotional balance. When these needs are not met, we experience emotions of distress, including anger. Persistent problems with anger imply unresolved psychological needs.

Of all the common human needs, the most obvious and important is the need for love. When we feel consistently loved, our emotions show it through their stability. But when we lack love, we respond to our rejected feelings with anger. Through anger we cry the unspoken question, *Why can't you just love me?*

John sought counseling at the encouragement of his wife because of his ongoing problems with depression. He was thirty-eight years old and had just transferred to a new job in town. "I've been in the banking

> **Persistent problems with anger imply unresolved psychological needs.**

industry for the past fifteen years, and lately things have been rough," he said. "We've been through so much turmoil lately, no one is ever certain a job is secure. I guess that's why I've been feeling down."

His wife, Judy, had read books on depression and had learned that depression is closely linked to anger. She had noticed John's tendency to hide his feelings under a pretense that all was well. But she knew by his chronic ulcer problems he was carrying a heavy emotional load. He seemed tense and edgy much of the time. In their initial interview Judy told Dr. Carter, "I'll tell you what's wrong because John won't admit it. He's angry. But he keeps it all inside, and it turns into depressed moodiness."

"I wouldn't call it anger," John replied, "but I will admit to feeling frustrated or hurt quite a bit." Turning to Dr. Carter, he asked, "Feeling frustrated isn't the same as feeling angry, is it?"

Dr. Carter responded, "Actually there are many shades of anger, and frustration is one of them. You don't have to be a wild man to feel angry. Anger can be experienced as disappointment or hurt or depression."

Next they discussed how anger could be identified in John's lifestyle. "I'm curious to know how long you've been struggling with your emotions," Dr. Carter inquired, realizing John's depression was linked to more than just his current job situation.

"I guess you could say I've had problems off and on for most of my life. Things haven't always been easy for me."

"His dad was an alcoholic, who finally died about seven years ago," Judy interjected. "It's as though John grew up never knowing his father. His dad was always off drinking with his buddies."

John nodded, "That's right. And Mom was so preoccupied with paying bills she didn't have much time for my sister and me. She was kind, but she was also tense and not very available to talk about personal matters. I struggled with insecurity for years."

As John shared more details of his childhood, Dr. Carter began to realize that the major need in his life, the need for love, remained woefully unmet. John had never been beaten or abused, although he had been forced to guard his behavior if his dad came home in a foul mood. Intellectually, he knew his parents loved him, yet little had been expressed during this childhood that made him feel truly loved.

A case such as John's easily illustrates that insufficient love creates fertile ground for emotional instability. We do not have to stretch our imaginations to guess that John gradually became weary of feeling left out of his parents' lives. He wanted affirmation but did not know how to find it. He also became hypersensitive to any hint that others might not care about him either. In marriage and even in his career, he often interpreted others' differences as rejection. Quietly, he stored his anger until it created a sour disposition that eventually turned into full depression.

We often think our love needs would have been met if we had a history of being hugged and told, "I love you." Certainly this can communicate warm affection, but love involves much more. Notice in the following examples how love can be communicated to developing children:

- Time is spent in friendly conversations about activities of the day.
- When discipline is administered, it is accompanied by an even tone of voice.
- Critical remarks are set aside in favor of reassurance and compliments.
- Time is spent together in reading or singing.
- When major decisions are considered, the child's point of view is openly solicited.
- There is ongoing encouragement to talk openly about personal feelings and delicate subjects.
- Routine directives can be given in a pleasant manner.
- Touching is done naturally and comfortably.

Each of these behaviors communicates love. Security is nurtured when these actions become habits. Think about your own childhood as you respond to the following statements.

Our family conversations were *(for instance, open and friendly; rare and stressful)* _____

When discipline was administered in our home, I felt *(for instance, sad, but still loved; afraid and humiliated)* _____

I used to wish my parents would be more interested in *(for instance, my basketball games; spending more time together outdoors on weekends)*

_____

Touch in our family was *(for instance, frequent and comfortable; rare and uncomfortable)* _____

In family decisions my opinions were *(for instance, nonexistent; valued)*

_____

■ ■ ■ ■

No family is perfect, so it is normal to admit that your love needs sometimes were not satisfied. In fact, if you proclaim that your needs were *always* met, you probably have idealized your past.

The more you struggle with anger, the more it indicates that some of your need for love was unmet. But let's not put all of the emphasis on parental love. Throughout life a wide array of relationships affect our emotional dispositions. Certainly our relationships with brothers and sisters are factors in feeling loved. Success in friendships also is important in knowing we are loved. And through the adult years marital satisfaction plays a great role in affirming the feeling of being loved.

In contrast, notice in the following illustrations how unfulfilled love in these relationships can feed anger.

■ A single woman in her thirties is envious because most of her friends are married with children. She struggles with anger because of her own history of broken dating relationships.

■ An adult woman frequently recalls how demeaning her brother was to her during their childhood. She is insecure at family gatherings and resentful that no one ever stood up to him.

A wife feels her husband is chronically edgy and easily annoyed, leaving her to wonder if he secretly wishes he had married someone else.

A man who has felt rejected by a group of his peers feels angry because he had tried hard to be friendly, but to no avail.

■ ■ ■ ■

Unresolved rejection can be harmful by keeping anger alive. Respond to the following statements:

I would describe the love between my siblings and myself as _____

_____

I am most disappointed with my friends when _____

If I could change something about my dating or marital relationship I would change _____

■ FEELING UNLOVED BREEDS DEPENDENCY

All humans share a trait that becomes a problem when love needs go unmet. It is the trait of dependency. Dependency allows inner thoughts and emotions to be dictated by external circumstances. When our needs for love are balanced, we are less dependent, but when our love needs are unmet, our dependencies increase, making us more vulnerable to anger.

To determine your tendencies toward dependency, check the appropriate following statements that apply to you.

☐ While speaking to others I wonder if I am saying things the right way.

☐ When someone else is disagreeable, I tend to become edgy and disagreeable too.

☐ I hide my flaws from others because maintaining a good image is important to me.

☐ I become guarded if I am with a strong-willed person.

☐ Sometimes I adjust my behavior because I know it will make me more popular, at least for awhile.

☐ I make plans to feel composed, but those plans are easily altered when others are tense.

☐ When someone disagrees with me, I try to convince him or her of my point of view.

☐ I become impatient if I have to let someone complete a project differently from the way I would do it.

☐ I can lose sight of my good intentions if someone acts incompetently.

☐ I have a real need to be accepted by others.

If you checked five or more of these statements, you probably let your emotional stability depend too heavily on others. This can make you prone to anger.

Many ask, Is it wrong to be dependent? The answer is no. Dependency is present in every personality, with no exceptions. And it is there for good reasons. Dependency is the glue that holds relationships together. *Imbalanced* dependency is the situation we want to avoid.

Each of us screamed and cried as we entered the world. We wanted to be held, nurtured, and loved—evidence of our innate tendency toward dependency. During infancy we felt satisfied when we received consistent nurturing and protection. Our inner security was clearly shaped by the people surrounding us.

As we progressed through childhood our dependency became less pronounced, yet it was still apparent. We felt secure when loving exchanges occurred in our homes, and we felt afraid when rejection was felt. As we matured into teenagers, our dependencies became increasingly social. We wanted to be accepted by our peers; we wanted to be "in." And dependency did not cease once we crossed into adulthood. As adults we want to be loved by the opposite sex. We want acceptance for our achievements. As parents, we want our children to think well of us. We want to belong to the community.

Dependency never ceases to influence our personalities. Seen in its best light, it keeps us tied to relationships and makes companionship work. Its downside is that dependency can cause us to be "reactors" who are prone to anger. Specifically, when your anger is too powerful, it implies you have concluded that you cannot be emotionally stable as long as the people or circumstances in front of you do not satisfy.

As John worked with Dr. Carter to understand his depression and its underlying anger, he became increasingly aware of his tendency to let his emotional stability depend on others.

"When I first started examining my emotions, I thought my problems were just caused by my career unrest," he said. "But now I'm seeing there is a much bigger picture to explore. I've had bruised emotions for years because I yearned for someone to affirm me."

"So, consciously or not, you concluded that you could not be emotionally secure until you received the reinforcement you so deeply craved from others," Dr. Carter reflected.

"You're exactly right," John nodded. "But how could I have lived so long without seeing this?"

"You're not alone in that respect," Dr. Carter reassured him. "Most people do not recognize their dependencies because they have not been trained to examine their emotions carefully."

Ideally, as children develop they should first feel secure that their parents, family, and friends love them unconditionally. Then, as they mature they should be trained to contemplate independently how they will handle their many emotions. For example, a nine-year-old girl who is irritated by her brother's teasing can be asked, "What options do you have when your brother treats you this way?"

Realistically, most people are not encouraged to think through the meaning of their emotions. So, like John, they tend to let their emotions depend on their circumstances. This is dangerous because no circumstances can possibly produce the exact ingredients for anyone's emotional stability.

What about you? In your developmental years, how much were you encouraged to contemplate the meaning of your emotions? Answer the following questions.

■ ■ ■ ■

When your dad would notice you were struggling with emotions, how would he respond? *(For instance, he was uncomfortable with my feelings so he would quickly tell me what to do.)*

_____

_____

_____

_____

How about your mother? How would she respond to your emotions? *(For instance, she seemed very busy, and I never wanted to disturb her by talking about personal things.)*

_____

_____

_____

_____

What about your brothers and sisters? Were you able to share your feelings satisfactorily with them? *(For instance, my sister was too self-centered to care about my feelings.)*

_____

_____

_____

_____

And your friends? Could you share your emotions with them? *(For instance, I had a best friend who would talk with me, but many times our discussions became gossip sessions.)*

_____

_____

_____

_____

And in your adult years, how satisfied are you in feeling understood by another adult? *(For instance, I'm divorced, and I feel like an outsider when I'm with other adults my age who are married.)*

_____

_____

_____

_____

■ ■ ■ ■ ■

John freely acknowledged to Dr. Carter, "I can't remember anyone *ever* encouraging me to explore the meaning of my emotions. Thinking back, I guess my emotions have always been at the disposal of anyone who played a major role in my life. No wonder I've felt so fragile."

"Your depression and anger have been caused by your craving for love and your lack of initiative to find out how you would fare if you didn't receive that love," Dr. Carter reflected. "I guess it's time for us to determine if you can adjust your historical patterns so you are not so tied to others' whims. Are you ready to look at your alternatives?"

"I sure am," said John. "It's time I started planning my emotions more carefully rather than letting my stability hinge on others' approval."

"Great," affirmed Dr. Carter. "We'll start by looking at two factors that will help you in your growth. The first is spiritual well-being, and the second is contemplative thinking."

■ BALANCING YOUR DEPENDENCIES

Many people can relate to John's history of an unmet need for love. They know their anger, distasteful though it may be, has become a habit, and they need an unnatural inner strength to help them break free from their pain. This happens when dependency on humans is exchanged for a dependency on strength from God. It sounds so simple. But balancing your dependencies is easier said than done.

Developing Spiritual Well-Being

In Chapter 1 we defined anger and discussed how it can be linked to an unfulfilled need for worth or respect. And we noted how this need can be met by accepting God's great declaration of our worth. Now let's take that idea a step further by examining what it means to have a deeply rooted sense of spiritual well-being. Such a change, by the way, is not gained by mere knowledge alone. We find it only as we appeal to God for the transforming work of His Holy Spirit and pray regularly for His intervention.

> "The heart is deceitful above all things, and desperately wicked; who can know it?"
> —Jeremiah 17:9

First, to find spiritual well-being we must acknowledge the unreliability of humans. This is not meant to encourage a critical or cynical view of our family and friends. Instead it encourages us to accept the ugly reality of sin. In unflattering terms, Jeremiah 17:9 warns, "The heart is deceitful above all things, and desperately wicked; who can know it?"

■ ■ ■ ■

If you acknowledge the unreliability of humans, how could you alter your thoughts when you are disappointed with someone's unwillingness to be loving? *(For instance, when my father continues to belittle my ideas, I will remind myself that he has never taken the time to contemplate his relational goals as I have.)*

1. _____

   _____

2. _____

   _____

■ ■ ■ ■

Second, spiritual well-being occurs as we acknowledge our own inability to solve all our problems. Romans 8:8 tells us "those who are in the flesh cannot please God." This means when we attempt to stabilize our emotions through our own efforts, we simply do not have what it takes to find His peace. In contrast, as we admit our weaknesses we take a step toward personal stability.

At this point we are ready for the third element of spiritual well-being: yielding our self-will to the will of Christ and letting our lives be guided by His wisdom.

■ ■ ■ ■

How can acknowledging your ineptness and your need for Christ's empowerment make a difference in your anger? (*For instance, when my wife invalidates my opinions, I can remind myself that, even though my natural instinct is to fight unfairly, I am committed to letting the Lord guide me with patience.*)

1. _____

_____

2. _____

_____

■ ■ ■ ■

Finally, as we develop spiritual well-being, we choose to endorse the healthy characteristics prescribed in God's Word. We set boundaries and act assertively when necessary (as described in Chapter 2). Then we resolve to develop a godly reputation. This distinction is made in Galatians 5:19–23, which clearly contrasts the "works of the flesh" in those who live in emotional disarray with the traits epitomizing the "fruit of the Spirit."

Works of the Flesh	Fruit of the Spirit
adultery, fornication, uncleanness, lewdness, idolatry, sorcery, hatred, contentions, jealousies, outbursts of anger, selfish ambitions, dissensions, heresies, envy, murders, drunkenness, revelries	love, joy, peace, longsuffering, kindness, goodness, faithfulness, gentleness, self-control

Some circumstances tempt us to lose our focus and succumb to ugly emotional expressions. Yet with a powerful commitment to composure we can focus on the fruit of the Spirit until it becomes habitual.

John, for example, realized that instead of harboring anger when he felt unappreciated by coworkers, he could commit to a plan of action consistent with the fruit of the Spirit. Later he told Dr. Carter, "I recognize it is my choice either to be driven by others' feelings toward me or by my own commitment to the Lord."

"That's a major insight," said Dr. Carter. "Can you give me an example of this?"

"Sure," answered John. "A man in my office is very critical, and I have had to work with him on a major project. A couple of days ago he snapped at me because I had not included all of his ideas in a report I had written. In the past, I would have sulked for the rest of the day, then made life miserable for Judy once I got home. But I decided my mood did not have to depend on his feelings. I realized his insecurity caused him to be so insistent. Rather than nursing a simmering anger, I knew the Lord wanted me to be gentle. So I was firm in standing my ground, but I didn't get caught in his emotional games."

"You actually thought that quickly about your emotional dependencies and choices?" asked Dr. Carter.

"Yes, I really did. I've discovered that once I identify potential situations of dependency I can readily plan how I will be used in those times by the Lord. Awareness is the key."

■ ■ ■ ■

How about you? Think about some times when you might apply the traits of the Holy Spirit rather than the traits of unhealthy anger. When could you yield to peacefulness rather than succumb to a sour disposition? *(For instance, when I take a break from my work, I can appreciate the few moments of rest rather than spending those minutes griping about the work still ahead.)*

_____

_____

.

When could you show patience rather than irritability? *(For instance, when my son asks me for the fourth time if he can invite a friend to the house, I can speak firmly yet remember he is still just a child who sometimes is overeager.)*

How about self-control? In which situations are you vulnerable to losing self-control? *(For instance, when I am explaining a task to my wife, I can recognize that she does not have the same mechanical aptitude I have, and I can choose to keep irritation out of my voice when she asks simple questions.)*

■ ■ ■ ▢

Breaking dependency patterns requires us to anticipate situations that make us vulnerable to anger. While we cannot expect to know what lies in the future, we can remember that we are not obligated to be reactors only. We can learn to initiate healthy behavior with a mind fixed on God's traits.

"A point to remember," Dr. Carter told John, "is that you may not be able to exhibit perfectly the fruit of the Spirit at all times for the rest of your life. But you can focus on how God will guide you through brief increments of time. For example, you may find it hard to imagine being patient forever with that critical coworker, but when you know you are about to confer with him, you can commit to an hour's worth of patience."

"I'm glad to hear you say that, because it makes my task less overwhelming," John replied.

"A spiritually grounded life is not the result of a onetime decision," said Dr. Carter. "Rather, we need to decide each day, sometimes several times each day, how we will yield to God's empowerment. In a sense we 'sign up' again and again to be anchored in Him."

Developing a Contemplative Mind

We have said that the first step toward balanced dependency is developing spiritual well-being. But to make this trait a powerful reality a contemplative mind is also required. It is not enough to know *what* spiritual traits you want. You need to explore *why* you want them in the first place. This can help you "own" those traits in a very personal way.

For example, many people are stuck in their anger despite knowing what the Christian life looks like; this happens because their Christianity is only dutiful performance. They are not truly motivated to live in spiritual strength. John once told Dr. Carter, "I've been told for years that Christians should be kind in the wake of someone else's rudeness. But I've never liked the sound of the instruction, 'Just do it.' It seemed too cut-and-dried for me."

> When we contemplate the meanings of our behavior, godly traits become purposeful rather than perfunctory.

"John, if you're like me, you probably don't like being told to do something just because someone says that's the best thing to do," said Dr. Carter. "You want your behavior to have real meaning."

"That's right. I might hear a preacher say I should live in Christ's love, but just because I am told to do it doesn't mean it will happen."

To be truly successful in depending on God, it is good, even necessary, to ask *why*. Why should I be forgiving? Why should I speak kindly?

Why would I want to respond to rejection with inner confidence? What difference does it make?

When we contemplate the meanings of our behavior, godly traits become purposeful rather than perfunctory. We are not just going through the motions but acting out of well-conceived convictions.

How about you? Have you taken the time to wrestle with the meaning of your Christian convictions? Do you like to study emotions? Do you regularly pause to talk with God about the motivations for your actions?

■ ■ ■ ■

Consider your tendencies by responding to the following questions:

Rather than expecting others to solve your problems, what could you do to take more responsibility for managing your emotions? *(For instance, I could spend less time complaining about my frustrations and more time reading books that show me the way to be balanced.)*

_____

_____

_____

_____

Do you have a friend who lets you think out loud about your emotional plans? What occurs in these conversations? *(For instance, I have a friend who listens quietly when I talk, then patiently prompts me to sift out my options.)*

_____

_____

_____

_____

What about your spouse or other members of your extended family? How could you work together to create an atmosphere more conducive to emotional contemplation? *(For instance, my spouse and I have agreed to set aside time each Thursday evening to discuss family matters of the week.)*

_____

_____

_____

_____

■ ■ ■ ■

Contemplative thinking leads to this conclusion: *In the Lord I have competence. I do not have to be pulled down by others' behavior.* Notice how contemplative thinking differs from dependency in the following comparisons.

Dependency: *I worry about how others will treat me.*
Contemplation: *I may want to be liked by others, but I can manage just fine even if others don't think as I do.*

Dependency: *I'm not sure I can handle adversity.*
Contemplation: *If problems arise, somehow I'll manage them.*

Dependency: *My anger is driven by temporary emotional impulses.*
Contemplation: *My anger is guided by well-conceived beliefs.*

Dependency: *I've got to have steady surroundings so I can be stable.*
Contemplation: *I like steady surroundings, but I can learn how to remain steady even in the midst of unrest.*

Knowing you can draw upon spiritual strength, you can choose not to let your anger be at the mercy of your environment.

4

▪▪ Feeling Controlled
Causes Anger

▪ Step 4. Choose to relinquish your cravings
for control in exchange for freedom.

Melanie, a tall, middle-aged woman with shoulder-length auburn hair, spoke with Dr. Minirth about her history of anxiety attacks. "I seem to have continual frustration in my daily activities, but I can't put my finger on the reasons why. Sometimes I feel so stressed I get short of breath and my chest feels tight. It's so traumatic I think I'm suffocating."

Dr. Minirth asked Melanie several questions about her overall health, then, making an educated guess, he asked, "Would you tell me what makes you angry?"

"Angry?" she asked as if her secret had just been exposed. "Well, uh, yes, you might say I feel that way sometimes. But I haven't really put much thought into what specifically makes me angry."

Actually, Melanie was hedging. She had a long laundry list of problems that fed her anger. But she had grown up in a very restrictive environment that discouraged open admission of imperfections. So Dr. Minirth had to prod a bit. "We all feel frustration from time to time, so anger is nothing to be afraid to admit," he said. "What frustrates you?"

Melanie spoke sheepishly at first, but she became more forceful as the words flowed. "We have a twenty-four-year-old son living at home who refuses to grow up. I've pleaded with my husband, Gary, to do something to get him out from under our roof. But honestly, Gary is the most stubborn man I know. I couldn't get through to him if I shouted through a megaphone. He's the master of his own ship, and I'm just expected to fall in line with his wishes. Our son knows he can get away with being lazy because Gary won't lift a finger to make him work!"

As she spoke, red blotches broke out on her neck.

Dr. Minirth quietly replied, "And you've tried throughout your marriage to communicate your feelings to Gary but with little luck, right?"

She nodded. Thinking about the tension in her home caused Melanie's blood pressure to rise.

For the next twenty minutes she and Dr. Minirth discussed the things that made her angry. One problem was that Gary refused to get along with Melanie's extended family members. But she admitted she felt tense around them, too, because they were so quick to offer unsolicited advice. She also had problems with several women friends because they didn't contribute as much to the relationships as she did. Another problem was that she and Gary had accumulated thousands of dollars of credit card debts, mostly for nonessential items, and now they were being advised to file for bankruptcy. Melanie summarized her situation by saying, "There's nothing in my world that fits my preferences. Everywhere I turn I feel controlled by something I can do absolutely nothing about!"

I feel controlled. Those three words cut to the heart of Melanie's anger. Seemingly deprived of the God-given privilege to choose for herself, Melanie was being controlled by people and circumstances. This kind of imprisonment by a controlling environment is a major factor that creates anger.

Have you ever experienced this kind of helplessness? Perhaps your external situations vary from Melanie's, but you can relate to the emotion that builds when you realize someone else is calling the shots and you can do little to get back into the driver's seat.

No human was created to be controlled by another. As schoolchildren all of us were undoubtedly taught that freedom is a gift to be cherished. We learned to love and respect our country as the lighthouse of liberty. As we matured we also learned the value of cooperation and compromise within our families, marriages, friendships, workplaces, and churches. But sometimes that cooperation is replaced by unreasonable demands by people or institutions. These demands can cause us to feel controlled, and that leads to anger.

To determine the level at which you may have been controlled, check the following items that apply to you.

- ☐ When I grew up, I was expected to obey the rules with no questions asked.

- ☐ I would like to speak more freely about personal matters, but to do so would only lead to arguments or disappointments.

- ☐ When I share a unique opinion or preference, it is often met with a putdown or an invalidation.

- ☐ The people I'd like to be most open with are too unavailable to me.

- ☐ I feel as if I live in the midst of critics.

- ☐ Peacefulness only seems to come when I can get away by myself.

- ☐ I often calculate in advance the way I will use my words.

- ☐ Some of my closest relationships have been soured by long stretches of silence and no communication.

- ☐ I often feel that my performances are all that matters to others.

- ☐ I have close relationships that could best be described as stressful.

If you checked five or more items, you probably are susceptible to easy anger, and your environment may have a rigidity that makes emotional composure difficult.

Controlling behavior is shown in a variety of ways. The most obvious ways are bossiness, criticism, stubbornness, dogmatic communication, and chronic rebuttals. But control is an extremely broad-based trait; it can also be shown by unavailability, silence, apathy, fretting, and ultrasensitivity.

As Melanie talked with Dr. Minirth, she admitted, "Every time I think about my family, a knot tightens in my stomach. Frankly, I can't remember ever *not* feeling controlled. Dr. Minirth, I'm a mature woman with grown children, yet it seems no one will give me credit for having normal ideas or legitimate feelings. Sometimes I could just scream!"

Dr. Minirth explained, "Your anger, then, is a way of communicating, *Please, let me be me*. Through anger you are protesting the fact that others place such little trust in you."

"You can say that again," said Melanie. "But as hard as I try, I still can't get anyone to understand what you just said. I wish I knew why others have to be so controlling."

◼ WHY CONTROL OCCURS

Control is not always bad. After all, we do need organization and structure to maintain peace in our lives. But excessive control creates more negatives than positives. Why are people too controlling? Three factors stand out: (1) performance takes priority over relationships, (2) differentness is threatening, and (3) obligation is taught as being mandatory rather than a choice. Let's look at each of these factors separately.

Performance Takes Priority

Think about your communication with others. When problems surface or emotions appear, what tends to happen? If your experiences are like most people's, performance or actions, rather than feelings or perceptions, become the focus for control virtually every time. Notice the following situations:

- A ten-year-old girl has difficulty handling her mathematics assignment. She is obviously frustrated and near tears. Her teacher responds by saying, "You can't expect to get your work done by just sitting there. If it seems too hard, try to remember what I taught you this morning."

- A wife's schedule has disintegrated because of constant interruptions. At the end of the day she recounts her irritations to her husband, who responds by saying, "You need to write down your daily schedule and stick to it. That way you'll have fewer days like today."

A man is frustrated because some unexpected bills have cut into his monthly budget. A friend hears about the problem and says, "Why don't you just throw away your credit cards? That helped me."

■ ■ ■ ■

Each of these examples contains seemingly innocent responses to a common lifestyle situation. A problem occurs, prompting some friendly advice from another person. That seems perfectly fine, right? But notice what is missing in each of the previous illustrations: no one is willing to talk about feelings or personal perceptions. When an emotion-laden circumstance arises, we immediately address performance, not emotion. Personal feelings are pushed aside. The result is a feeling of being controlled.

Can you think of a common example when your feelings might be ignored as proposed solutions are pushed at you? *(For instance, if I tell my wife about a problem at work she will tell me how to handle it, ignoring my feelings about it.)*

1. _____

_____

2. _____

_____

■ ■ ■ ■

Occasionally there may be times we feel relieved when someone shows us how we could manage our problems. But usually we are left feeling empty because we had hoped for a listening ear rather than unsolicited advice. When this pattern is chronically repeated, we feel stepped on and disrespected.

In Matthew 22:35–39 a conversation is recorded between Jesus and a young lawyer who had asked Him to cite God's greatest commandment. Jesus' familiar reply was, "'You shall love the Lord your God with all your heart, with all your soul, and with all your mind.' This is the first and great commandment. And the second is like it: 'You shall love your neighbor as yourself.'" In that succinct statement Jesus reminded His listeners that relating in love—first with God, then with others—is the ultimate goal in life.

Relating in love means personal, intimate matters take first priority. Performance is not insignificant, but it is not the essence of who we are. What we feel, how we think, what we perceive, these elements are at the core of our identities. So if our relationships are to be successful, we must make room in our communication for the "internal" elements. With this in mind, let's look back at the three illustrations just mentioned:

> Relating in love means personal, intimate matters take first priority. Performance is not insignificant, but it is not the essence of who we are.

- When the ten-year-old girl is struggling with her mathematics, the teacher can say, "I know you'd like to master this project so you can get on to something else. That's why it's frustrating when it doesn't make sense. Tell me how you're feeling right now."

- As the husband listens to his wife describe her failed schedule he can respond, "Wow, when nothing goes as planned it makes you wonder where the day went. Sometimes it seems there aren't enough hours to manage everything that comes your way."

- The man whose friend complains about having too many bills can say, "It can give you a sinking feeling as you wonder how you're going to juggle your commitments."

When personal issues are addressed this way, the relationship takes priority over the performance. Control, then, is minimized while personal uniqueness is allowed.

■ ■ ■ ■

Can you think of some common instances when you could be more tuned in to another person's feelings? *(For example, as my friend tells me about a recent marital problem I can let her know that I care about the hurt she feels.)*

1. _____
   _____

2. _____
   _____

■ ■ ■ ■

Differentness Is Threatening

Most people consider themselves open-minded enough to allow others to be different, to be unique. In our counseling practices, however, we have found that while most people give themselves credit for being open-minded, their lives do not reflect this tolerance.

From the earliest years of childhood through late adulthood, people like familiarity. If you have ever spent a week out of town you probably remember the pleasant anticipation you felt when you returned home, looking forward to sleeping in your own bed again. We enjoy new and unique experiences, but lasting composure comes when we are able to reduce our world into familiar, recognizable patterns.

This tendency is most apparent in the way we relate to each other. Although we may not be consciously aware of it, we desperately want emotional and relational issues to be predictable. Notice this in the following examples:

- A husband tells his wife he is annoyed by their son's social activities. She invalidates his emotions when she responds, "I wish you wouldn't be so hard on our son. Just once it would be nice to hear you comment on something he does right."

- A single man tells a friend he wants to quit his job and look for an entirely new line of work. The friend says, "Don't you think it's a big risk to uproot yourself when you've already got a good life?"

- A woman confides to a coworker that she is having trouble in her marriage. The coworker replies, "Of all the people I know, you're the one who's capable of getting over this. All marriages have bad stretches."

In each of these illustrations the person who expresses an intimate feeling or desire is answered with the perceived response, *Don't think that way; it's too different!* Although the respondents probably intend to be encouraging, their "tie-it-down" communication indicates a need for predictability.

People who struggle with anger often complain that they are required to guess the other person's hidden agenda and then conform to it. They have a history in which uniqueness, particularly emotional uniqueness, has been discouraged. "Be like us" has been the theme; "stay within the mold." Anger represents a protest against this stereotyping.

■ ■ ■ ■

Have you ever felt that others were trying to fit your feelings and perceptions into a prescribed format? What are some examples of this? *(For instance, my parents still insist that I should have the same religious practices as they do; my husband insists that I wear the colors of clothing he likes best.)*

1. _____

_____

2. _____

_____

When you sense that others do not want you to stray from their mold, how does this affect your anger? *(For instance, on the outside I try to appear compliant, but inwardly I have a secret desire to run.)*

1. _____

_____

2. _____

_____

■ ■ ■ ■

Harmony among difference is part of God's ingenious design. He does not intend everyone and everything to be the same; instead we are to blend our uniqueness in complementary ways. This is shown in the variety of colors, sights, sounds, animals, plants, feelings, faces, and personalities that exist throughout His creation. It is this variety that gives richness to our experiences. A lack of differences would create a truly miserable world.

With this in mind, think of the healthiness represented by others' differentness rather than feeling forced to conform to their impositions.

■ ■ ■ ■

What good comes from your uniqueness? *(For instance, I'm more emotional than my spouse, so I am also capable of communicating empathy when my children feel upset.)*

1. _____

_____

2. _____

_____

■ ■ ■ ■

No apology is required when differentness is evident. Your only task is to be certain you are living in a way that is sensitive to others' uniqueness.

Obligation Is Perceived as Mandatory

A third reason for controlling behavior relates to a history of obligation rather than choice. Controlled people can invariably recall instructions about how they were to speak and act. Yet they draw mental blanks when asked how they were trained to make their own choices affecting the structure of their lives.

For example, one controlling father told his son, "When I was a boy, we didn't foolishly squander our time playing video games. We learned the value of a good day's work." When the boy asked why he should follow that path, too, the dad said, "Because that's just the way it ought to be." The father was promoting a good behavior pattern, but his reasoning was shallow. The son felt frustration, not necessarily because he thought the behavior was wrong, but because he resented the mindless obligation that was being forced on him.

Controlling people are so interested in the bottom line they become intolerant of those who struggle with their own reasoning about the subject in question. To them, obligation is all that really matters. This may result in reliable task accomplishment, but it creates frustration in the relationship because it bypasses the other person's struggle to create a feeling of ownership for the behavior. Examples abound:

- A father tells a daughter she has to help with kitchen chores. No questions are allowed. "Just do it."

- A wife gripes that her husband should take a greater interest in their son's school work because it is his obligation to be an involved parent.

- A young woman feels she must always be available for her best friend's needs because it would seem nonsupportive if she had separate activities involving someone else.

- A teenager knows he had better go to church because his family expects it of him.

While we all need (and even like) structure in our lives, we struggle with anger when others insist that we blindly follow their rule book.

■ ■ ■ ■

What are some examples of obligations that have been imposed upon you? *(For instance, my husband thinks it is the wife's obligation to buy all the family's Christmas presents; my mother expects me to spend every Saturday morning chauffeuring her on her errands.)*

1. _____

_____

2. _____

_____

■ ■ ■ ■

Why do we resent obligatory impositions? Although the controlling person may not consciously intend it, the message he or she conveys is,

You're not trustworthy. Controlling people believe if choices are eliminated then the chance for irresponsibility can be erased as well.

Dr. Minirth and Melanie discussed how she had felt controlled. "You know, Dr. Minirth, I've felt tense with Gary because I've always had this sense that he wants to hold me to his agenda," she said.

"So you expended all sorts of energy trying to guess what dictates he might throw at you next?"

"That's right. He expects so much of me that I feel like I'm little more than a machine to him. And what is worse, if I try to express my feelings about this, it's as if I'm talking to a stone wall. He doesn't care about me."

"You interpret his control as a lack of caring, and that interpretation sparks the anger," Dr. Minirth reflected. "When the anger arises, how do you handle it?"

"I'm afraid that's where my problem begins," said Melanie. "Sometimes I just suppress it, but other times I explode and become irrational. Often I take it out on other people, and that doesn't help matters at all."

RESPONDING TO OTHERS' CONTROL

Melanie was beginning to understand that her anger was linked to the frustration of being controlled; but she still needed to find a better way of handling her response to it. Her discussions with Dr. Minirth then turned to (1) her tendency to counter-control and (2) acknowledging her freedom to be free.

Counter-Control

Clearly, it is unproductive to be controlled by another person. But too often we respond to this unproductive control with our own inappropriate reaction. Anger makes us particularly susceptible to this response. Another person's attempt to control us is an invitation to a power play, and we often accept that invitation by engaging in our own counter-control tactics.

Dr. Minirth suggested to Melanie, "I can appreciate how you would want to sidestep Gary's control. But you seem to throw fuel on the fire by responding with your own brand of control."

"I know," she said with frustration. "I wish I could stop myself, but something comes over me and I get hooked into emotional warfare."

"Then the net result is that your anger escalates and anxiety gains a foothold," Dr. Minirth said as Melanie nodded.

Do you ever respond to someone's control with counter-control? Check the following statements that apply to you.

- ☐ When someone is being unfair, I consider it my responsibility to correct that unfairness.

- ☐ I openly argue with a family member or close associate who is stubborn.

- ☐ I may stew for hours after someone has acted unkindly toward me.

- ☐ I feel compelled to point out the illogic I hear in someone else's statement.

- ☐ I can be very uncooperative with someone who treats me unfavorably.

- ☐ Once someone has shown his or her "ugly side," I want to have little association thereafter.

- ☐ When confronted by a strong-willed debater, I respond with silence and defiant resistance.

- ☐ I am determined that no one can get away with telling me what to do.

- ☐ I often respond to another person's control with questions like, "Why do you have to . . . ?"

- ☐ When I have lost an argument, I grumble about the other person.

If you responded to five or more of these items, you are a likely candidate for ongoing power plays, and you probably have recurrent struggles with anger.

The desire to get away from another's control is both understandable and normal. However, when we accomplish this by using force, we add to the very atmosphere we dislike.

The familiar words of Proverbs 15:1 tell us, "A soft answer turns away wrath, but a harsh word stirs up anger." This does not mean we have to be subject to or enable abusive or controlling behavior. Rather, it means we can choose to behave appropriately in the face of another's inappropriateness. (By the way, it is possible to be firmly assertive while still maintaining a reputation of gentleness.)

> A soft answer turns away wrath, but a harsh word stirs up anger.
> —Proverbs 15:1

Can you think of any behavior that would benefit from a noncontrolling response from you? (*For example, when my husband speaks critically, I can truly listen to him and save my counter-remarks for a better time.*)

1. _____
   _____

2. _____
   _____

3. _____
   _____

By sidestepping the temptation to enter a power play, what advantages could you expect? (*For instance, we would not have as many "cold-as-ice" evenings in our home; I would not be as vulnerable to eventual explosions or temper tantrums.*)

1. _____
   _____

2. _____
   _____

When we resolve not to respond to a wrong with a wrong, we exercise personal responsibility. We also show ourselves to be less dependent on human input and more dependent on God's guidance.

ACKNOWLEDGING FREEDOM

To break the grip of another person's control and to refrain from becoming controlling ourselves, we can acknowledge God's declaration of freedom. God's scheme for proper living begins with this privilege. In fact, He declared our freedom in the first sentence He spoke to Adam. As God explained to Adam the rules of the garden, He said, "Of every tree of the garden you may freely eat; but of the tree of the knowledge of good and evil you shall not eat" (Genesis 2:16–17). Many people pass by this crucial statement without understanding its powerful meaning. Let's get a full idea of the philosophy it conveys.

> To break the grip of another person's control and to refrain from becoming controlling ourselves, we can acknowledge God's declaration of freedom.

In His statement to Adam, God was explaining that each human is given freedom—the presence of choices. Freedom is indigenous to who we are. We do not have to beg for it, nor do we have to prove ourselves first. Whether we use it wisely or poorly, each person has free will. It is simply a part of what we are.

God also explained that freedom is best balanced by a submission to His declarations of right and wrong. And no humans are capable of making those determinations for themselves. This is what is meant in the instruction not to eat of "the tree of the knowledge of good and evil." God is the One who should be in control. Humans are to refrain from the temptation to play God. When people are controlling, they ignore this most basic principle given at Creation. They are negating another's privilege of freedom and taking the position of God upon themselves.

So, as we seek victory over anger we would do well to follow this original principle: respond to another person's control with a mind-set of freedom. Examples of this can be found in everyday circumstances:

A wife is scolded by her husband because the house is not spotlessly clean. Rather than getting into a battle with him, she gives herself permission to clean the house in her own way, knowing she is a reasonable, responsible person. She also avoids a power play by acknowledging her husband's freedom to disagree.

A single man's roommate gives him unwanted advice about his need for increased social activity. The man acknowledges his roommate's right to an opinion but chooses to pursue his social life at his own pace, knowing he is responsible to God, not to his roommate.

An adult woman's mother expects her daughter to drop everything and cater to her demands. Realizing she cannot be responsible for her mother's trivial requests, the daughter is free to say no.

■ ■ ■ ■

Can you think of similar examples in your life when you could respond to control with freedom?

1. _____

_____

2. _____

_____

■ ■ ■ ■

There is always a risk that freedom can intermingle with selfishness to compound relationship problems. Yet that is a risk God is willing to take; therefore we, too, can recognize our freedom, even though it has potential hazards. (*For instance, a husband knows he is free, so he selfishly ignores his wife's legitimate requests to help with the children's activities.*)

As we respond to another person's control with a mind-set of freedom, it will be best to balance it with a sense of true responsibility. For example, that husband can help his wife with the children's activities, while also requesting that they each be allowed some time in the week just to relax with no pressures.

■ ■ ▨ ▨

Respond to the following thoughts.

Though other people want to control me, freedom means I can _____

_____

_____

_____

When living in freedom, my sense of responsibility will lead me to _____

_____

_____

_____

■ ■ ▨ ▨

Ideally, in freedom we choose to manage our anger by using one of the two healthy choices discussed in Chapter 2, assertiveness or dropping it. We are willing to set appropriate boundaries and state legitimate needs while also being wise enough to know when to be cooperative and noncontroversial.

Melanie's breakthrough came as she recognized that she did not have to remain stuck in anyone's control trap. She learned that as a free person she could choose to respond to her husband's control in any way she saw fit. To her credit, she chose to filter her anger through responsible means. For example:

 ▨ When Gary criticized her housekeeping, she calmly replied that she was doing the best she could. She suggested he pitch in to help if he felt more needed to be done.

 ▨ When her adult son asked for money, she told him she would be glad to help him financially after he first demonstrated financial responsibility with what he had.

 ▨ When her mother butted in with unwanted advice about her marriage, Melanie respectfully told her she would prefer to manage her problems without the criticism.

Melanie realized she could not stop other people from attempting to control her, but she learned she was free to sidestep their demands and make the choices she knew to be most responsible.

5

▪▪ Myths That
Perpetuate Anger

▪ Step 5. Ground yourself in truth by
setting aside idealistic myths.

Cindy's face betrayed her bewilderment. Her friends normally described her as perky and energetic, but now she felt weary. She admitted to Dr. Carter that she had been in an emotional tailspin for months. "You're the fourth counselor I've seen for my anger; maybe I'm wasting my time. Every time I try to get help we get bogged down in nonproductive talk about my early family and I leave feeling more frustrated than before I ever started counseling."

"Well, Cindy, I hope your experience here will prove to be more beneficial. Let's start by identifying the issues that brought you to my office."

Cindy explained that at age thirty-three she was ending her third marriage. In each case she had been "shafted," she said. She had married her first husband in college and had supported him while he tried to develop a music career. Her family had warned her he seemed too flaky, but she had ignored their cautions because she was strongly attracted to his free spirit. Within eighteen months she learned of his problem with chronic womanizing, and when he could not promise fidelity, she filed for divorce.

She told Dr. Carter, "I was so insecure then I felt like I was the guilty one. I felt I should have been able to satisfy him so he wouldn't wander."

She married again within two years and soon felt uneasy because of mysterious phone calls her new husband received from unidentified people. Whenever she asked about them, he would become enraged. Then she would quietly withdraw. Eventually she learned he led a secret life of homosexuality. After divorcing him she decided to "play it safe" by marrying a ministerial student. And even though he did not present the same problems, she left him after three years, claiming she couldn't "play his holiness games."

Cindy's anger was evident. Abruptly she told Dr. Carter, "I know you'll try to tell me differently, but I think all men are jerks! They only care about themselves, and when they're finished toying with a woman they'll dispose of her."

Dr. Carter considered the challenge ahead. Not only did he and Cindy need to make sense of her frayed emotions, they also had to eliminate the broad generalizations that fueled her anger. As long as she embraced such broad assumptions she could hardly be expected to incorporate godly truths into her mind-set.

Cindy was exhibiting a problem common to people caught in non-productive anger. She was utilizing *mythical thinking*, accepting as true a statement that is in fact false. For example, she had concluded that *all* men are "jerks," when in fact her experience was confined to three men.

■ ■ ■ ■

Have you ever fallen into the trap of mythical thinking? Try to recall a couple of times when this occurred. *(For instance, if my wife were more composed with the children we'd quit having problems at home; my job is so miserable it ruins every aspect of my life.)*

1. _____

_____

2. _____

_____

■ ■ ■ ■

Usually our mythical thoughts contain an element of truth. For example, Cindy truly had endured some poor experiences with men that would make anyone feel skittish. But when myths are stretched to the extreme, they lack logic and keep us from applying objective choices to our anger.

> To manage anger successfully we must eliminate false notions that perpetuate pain.

To manage anger successfully we must eliminate false notions that perpetuate pain. Listed below are several of the most common myths held by angry people.

MYTH 1. MY HISTORY OF REJECTION LEAVES ME EMOTIONALLY DEPLETED.

Because anger is so closely linked to experiences of rejection, it is common for angry people to assume they are forever jinxed if they have felt rejected several times. *No one will accept me,* this thinking goes, *so I've got every right to be angry.* Most of these people are realistic enough to know they cannot be accepted by all people at all times. But they are not prepared emotionally for the fact that several, even many people, may not accept them at all. So when rejections are repeated, hope fades while anger builds.

Cindy told Dr. Carter about her poor relationship with her father, who had been aloof. As a girl she had perceived that she was a nuisance to him. Her insecurities with him continued into her adult years, causing her to ache for male affection. But her feelings of inadequacy led her to choose men whose capacities for love were weak. This fed a pattern of loss, so she drew an understandable (though false) conclusion that she was worthless.

She told Dr. Carter, "I know lots of people who have been divorced once, but usually they make a much wiser selection the second time and life gets better. When a person gets a second divorce, it makes people wonder about what's wrong with him or her. But when you've been divorced three times like I have, it's the pits! I obviously don't do a good screening job when I meet a man. As a result I've been subjected to more than my fair share of rejection. It's more than I can handle."

Cindy's last statement, "It's more than I can handle," gave Dr. Carter an insight into her ongoing anger. On the surface Cindy was bemoaning the pain of her relationship failures, but the deeper issue was her belief in her own ineptitude. Like other angry people, Cindy had concluded she did not possess sufficient strength to withstand her past rejections, so she was stuck in the resulting mood of anger.

■ ■ ■ ■

When are you likely to assume that rejection eliminates your ability to maintain emotional composure? *(For instance, my father never complimented me, and now I cannot feel comfortable when a man shows me positive attention; when my wife ignores me, I lose my ability to work confidently with my business associates.)*

1. _____

_____

_____

2. _____

_____

_____

■ ■ ■ ■

We are told in 2 Timothy 1:7 that we *do* have the ability to thrive in spite of rejections: "For God has not given us a spirit of fear, but of power and of love and of a sound mind." From earliest childhood through adulthood we each have the capacity to rebound from rejection. We may not respond to those frustrations as perfectly as we would like, but we need not assume these rejections are final assessments.

■ ■ ■ ■

Go back to the illustrations you cited above. If you had been operating from an assumption that you can manage rejection, how would your thoughts have differed? *(For instance, although my father was not complimentary, if a man shows me positive attention I receive it with thanks; when my wife has ignored me, it does not mean I will have the same reaction from my business associates.)*

1. _____

_____

_____

2. _____

_____

_____

▪ MYTH 2. GOD SHOULD HAVE STOPPED MY PROBLEMS.

Anger is usually a by-product of some form of suffering. When we attempt to find the root of that suffering, we often blame God. For example, Cindy told Dr. Carter, "I was raised in a conservative church where we were taught to seek God's guidance. But I've concluded that all that teaching was a crock! Where was God when I needed Him? Why didn't He give me a better family? Why didn't He let me marry better men?"

"You seem to be giving God credit for choices made by humans," responded Dr. Carter. "Reading between the lines, it sounds like you wish God would have pulled strings for you rather than letting you be human."

Cindy wasn't convinced. "What I'm saying is that God knew what was going to happen to me. He could have stopped it. But instead He's letting me wallow in misery. It's not fair."

▪ ▪ ▪ ▪

When are you most prone to blaming God for your problems? *(For instance, I wish I could have been born to better parents, but apparently God thought otherwise.)*

1. _____

_____

_____

2. _____

_____

_____

■ ■ ■ ■

Because angry people feel as though they're backed into a corner of helplessness, it is common for them to frantically seek a shining knight who will make their problems go away. Knowing God is all powerful, many assume it is His job to put an end to their pain and suffering—right now! When He chooses not to intervene immediately in their tensions, it can be agonizing for them.

Check the following thoughts that have sometimes accompanied your anger.

- ☐ *A loving God could not possibly allow the torturous pain I have felt.*
- ☐ *If people reject me, it probably means God doesn't care about me either.*
- ☐ *God is too far away. He's not available when I need Him.*
- ☐ *God made a mistake when He allowed this to happen to me.*
- ☐ *I'm plagued with burdens that are simply too heavy to carry.*
- ☐ *My prayers seem to have no meaning. I'm not sure God hears them anyway.*

Statements like these are common to people who assume God owes them something. These thoughts feed a demanding mind-set that ultimately perpetuates ugly anger.

From the beginning of our existence God has respected free will. Even though it often causes humans to act totally counter to His ways, free will is such a major element in His design for human nature that He does not nullify it. In the short term (seventy-five years is very brief on God's calendar) free will often results in such confusing thoughts as those listed above. In the long term of eternity, though, we can be assured that suffering will be conquered. But angry people are by nature impatient; waiting for eternity to begin seems unreasonable.

To avoid getting bogged down in blaming God, you can refrain from all-or-nothing assumptions about His work in your life and about suffering. For example, Dr. Carter showed Cindy 1 Corinthians 4:7, which rhetorically asks, "What do you have that you did not receive?" He explained that this question is asked as part of a lesson that teaches us it is God Himself who gives us our coping skills, our wisdom, our inner strength. He told Cindy, "As I'm getting to know you I'm learning you have a lot of spunk. You've been knocked down but you still keep coming back. Although you may be tempted to assume God has completely abandoned you, I choose to believe He is responsible for the inner drive that causes you to keep bouncing back."

"I like the fact that you see my tenacity," she responded. "And you think it was given to me by God?"

"Where else does it come from?" asked Dr. Carter with a smile. "Let's see if you can channel the frustration you've aimed toward God into something more productive."

"Like what?" Cindy was definitely interested in this.

"Rather than griping that God has abandoned you, be thankful He has gifted you with an inquisitive mind. Then use that inquisitive mind to determine which kinds of people you need to befriend in the future."

"Sometimes my inquisitive mind causes me to appear cynical," reflected Cindy. "But considered in its most positive light, we could say it prompts me to learn how to meet my needs more adequately."

Dr. Carter added, "That's the point I want you to grasp. Your past experiences have caused pain. But they can also spur you toward a more clearly defined means of scrutinizing people. And that can become a plus."

"I see what you're getting at," replied Cindy. "Rather than assuming God is trying to make me feel miserable, I can acknowledge that He will help me turn my negatives into positives."

■ ■ ■ ■

How about you? How can you reinterpret frustrating events so you see God working with you? (*For instance, when my teenager acts rebellious, I will acknowledge that God can show me a more empathetic attitude toward other parents with similar problems.*)

1. _____

   _____

   _____

2. _____

   _____

   _____

■ MYTH 3. LETTING GO OF MY ANGER MEANS I AM CONCEDING DEFEAT.

In Chapter 2 we explored how choices can be applied to anger. On the positive side we discussed how we can assertively address issues related to worth, needs, and convictions. And when that proves fruitless, we still have the choice to drop the anger altogether, opting for forgiveness or acceptance of imperfection. But many angry people find this choice difficult. Richard was one of them. He checked into our hospital because of a prolonged episode of depression. He told Dr. Minirth that as a boy he had been repeatedly beaten by his father. Making matters worse, he had recently talked with his father about those incidents and the father had shrugged, saying he would not have beaten him if he had been obedient. With utter dejection, Richard sighed, "I've been told to forgive my father and lay the past to rest. But how can I? He shows no remorse, and I honestly believe if he had to do it all over again, he would mistreat me the same way with no sense of shame."

Dr. Minirth replied, "So letting go of your anger would seem like conceding defeat. In a sense you would be declaring him the winner."

"It may not be right to say so, but that's exactly the way it would feel," Richard answered.

■ ■ ■ ■

Have you ever endured circumstances that would not properly resolve? If so, you may be susceptible to a related myth that all misdeeds should be properly punished. List below two examples when you have thought this way. *(For instance, my husband still has not shown the necessary remorse after having an affair; my child just smirks at me after his punishment has ended.)*

1. _____

_____

_____

_____

2. _____

_____

_____

■ ■ ■ ■

Angry people feel like victims because of wrongs they have endured. In most cases those wrongs were uninvited and undeserved. But even someone like Cindy, whose problems were brought on by her own poor choices, will feel legitimately victimized because her pain was more intense than expected. Victimization causes angry people to conclude that forgiveness is unreasonable.

To overcome the defeated feeling that accompanies the wrongdoer's lack of change, we can confront ourselves with a very basic question: *Will my quality of life be greater if I choose to hold on to my anger rather than releasing it?* This question reminds us that we can drop our anger, not because another person has registered repentance but because it is the emotionally healthy choice. You may eventually conclude, *I still dislike the wrongs I've suffered, but I choose to thrive in spite of them.*

Check the statements you agree with.

☐ Others do not have to act correctly before I choose the proper direction for my anger.

☐ Choosing to drop my resentment is not the same as condoning wrong.

☐ I accept others' freedom to live in unhealthy ways.

☐ I accept the responsibility for my own emotions; others cannot force me to remain angry.

☐ Forgiveness and letting go of anger has nothing to do with winning or losing.

☐ It is not my duty to correct another person who chooses to gloat over his or her problems.

The more of these statements you can agree with, the more likely you are to lay harmful anger aside.

▰ MYTH 4. NO ONE UNDERSTANDS MY UNIQUE PROBLEMS.

During a particularly difficult session Cindy insisted that Dr. Carter could not possibly understand what she had experienced in the past several years.

"Cindy, what makes you so unsure I cannot grasp what you are feeling?" he asked. "You've done a good job explaining how you feel, and I can certainly identify with your pain. I hope you can appreciate that."

"I'll have to give you credit . . . you're a compassionate person. But you have a beautiful family who is there for you every day. I assume your family life isn't perfect, but you've never gone through the rejection of a divorce, much less three of them. Plus, you're a man. And men just don't experience their emotions the way women do."

"So who *does* understand you?"

She thought for a moment then said, "You really want to know? Nobody. I don't think anyone in my world can possibly imagine my humiliation. That's what keeps me so emotionally bogged down. It's bad enough to have experienced my losses, but I feel so all alone!"

If Cindy's assumption were correct, she could expect a future with little hope. Because we thrive on relational wholeness, a life without anyone to share a burden can be almost devoid of purpose.

■ ■ ▰ ▱

When have you felt that no one could understand your frustrating circumstances? *(For instance, in the past my finances were secure, but now I can't afford to go out to eat when friends invite me; in my social groups I seem friendly, but no one would believe the arguments that go on in my home.)*

1. _____
   _____
   _____

2. _____
   _____
   _____

■ ■ ■ ■

Fortunately, Cindy was not correct in her assessment of others. To assume her counselor or anyone else could not empathize without experiencing the same problems would be analogous to saying a physician had to be diseased before he or she could render healing comfort.

God has given humans a capacity to share another's hurt even though our experiences are not identical. For example, although Dr. Carter had not experienced the exact set of circumstances as Cindy, he knew what rejection and failure felt like. And by yielding himself to God, he could sense Cindy's emotions powerfully enough to make a warm personal connection. Cindy's problem was not that she was all alone. Instead, her anger had shielded her from the care she claimed to want.

To break the myth of her isolation and uniqueness, Cindy had to choose to acknowledge that someone with different experiences could still encourage her. Instead of focusing on the differences between her circumstances and other people's, she would focus on the fact that everyone knows disappointment in some form.

■ ■ ■ ■

How about you? Respond to the following sentences as you contemplate how you will let others befriend you in your moments of frustration.

When I am angry, I will not focus so much on my uniqueness that I cannot feel connected. Instead I will _____

_____

_____

When someone tells me about a problem similar to mine I can _____

_____

_____

■ ■ ■ ■

Most angry people have nursed their deepest feelings of pain in private, which feeds the myth that no one can understand them. But when they learn to be open about their needs and let others show concern, the anger gives way to feelings of relief. This means you will be willing to truly give up your anger rather than cling to it as Cindy did prior to her sessions with Dr. Carter.

> **Most angry people have nursed their deepest feelings of pain in private, which feeds the myth that no one can understand them.**

■ MYTH 5. I DON'T DESERVE TO BE HAPPY.

Several sessions into their work, Cindy revealed an interesting bit of information that helped explain her years of anger. She told Dr. Carter she had a younger sister whose problems seemed worse than her own.

"My sister Pamela is eight years younger than I am, and she's really had it rough. Our dad died when I was already married and out of the house, but she was only fourteen. Dad had been the disciplinarian, so when he was gone, Pamela went wild. She's been through numerous drug treatment programs. She's had two abortions. And I'll bet she couldn't count the number of men she's slept with. It's a pity to see how her life has unfolded."

"So how does this affect you, Cindy?" Dr. Carter asked. "I'm sure you must agonize over this."

"Well, it naturally holds me down. Every time I'm with her I'm reminded of how small my problems really are. At least I have my health and I have friends and a decent job. But she has nothing."

"Cindy, correct me if I'm wrong, but I perceive that you feel guilty for your sister's problems."

"Sometimes I really do. I've always felt I should have been a better role model for her, but instead I've been preoccupied with my own distractions. I've been so consumed with myself I never took the time to talk with her like a big sister should."

Expressing an intuition, Dr. Carter asked, "Could I assume if you began living a happy, contented life it would almost seem that you've abandoned Pamela?"

"In a strange way I *would* feel selfish," she admitted. "How can I feel right about being happy when she is in such misery?"

It is common to experience emotions as dictated by the norms of a group such as the family, a church, a workplace, or one's social circle. Almost subconsciously we put out "sensors" to determine what others are feeling; then we resolve to maintain our own emotions consistent with those of the group. This explains why it is easy to swap complaint for complaint or to respond to a funny story with a funny story.

■ ■ ■ ■

Think of some circumstances in your life that have held you to your anger. *(For instance, my brother has problems with his kids, and it causes me to openly complain about similar problems with my own.)*

1. _____

   _____

2. _____

   _____

■ ■ ■ ■

As noble as Cindy's loyalty was to her sister, she had allowed herself to be unnecessarily weighed down by outside pressures. She had accepted the myth that her own happiness would be harmful to Pamela. Dr. Carter helped her understand that all of us are responsible for rising above our own anger-producing circumstances, even if others choose to remain in their own problems. He helped her see how she could show empathy for her sister's struggles while enjoying success in resolving her own problems.

■ ■ ■ ▪

Respond to the following sentence as you think about how you can find recovery in spite of another's troubles.

When someone tells me about his or her problems, instead of joining in with complaint I can _____

_____

■ ■ ■ ▪

We need not feel compelled to take responsibility for others' problems, nor do we have to be sojourners with them in their misery. Instead we can view our efforts at managing our anger as a responsible contribution to the well-being of those who play important roles in our lives.

■ MYTH 6. THERE IS NOTHING TO LOOK FORWARD TO ANYMORE.

Momentum plays a powerful role in the way we handle emotions. For example, consider the role of momentum in athletics. When a team has a history of winning, a tradition grows that sparks the motivation of the players. They inwardly believe they are winners, and they assume as they give their best efforts to each game, the tradition will continue. Likewise, when a team has a tradition of losing, a negative mind-set builds as the players assume that victory will elude them again as it has in the past.

This same mind-set can work in anger management. When people have a pattern of irritations and irritability, it is easy for them to conclude that the future will be no different. Angry people can be so tied to their angry pattern they falsely conclude that corrective efforts would only be futile.

■ ■ ■ ▪

Have you ever had times when your anger was perpetuated by negative momentum? *(For instance, my husband and I disagree so frequently that I develop a sour disposition whenever I know we are going to spend time together.)*

1. _____

   _____

2. _____

   _____

■ ■ ■ ■

To inject some hope into his counseling sessions with Cindy, Dr. Carter challenged her. "I'm convinced that you have the capacity to make better choices when your anger arises. But you need to believe this too."

Cindy wanted to be convinced of this, but she asked, "Don't you think the best indicator of my future potential is my past failures? Because I've made so many mistakes, I can't afford to be optimistic."

Undaunted, Dr. Carter replied with a smile, "You know, if I spoke as pessimistically to you as you speak to yourself, you'd fire me! You've fallen into the habit of letting yourself remain angry, yet your presence here in my office tells me you're ready for an improvement.

"Besides," he continued, "you can tell the most about people, not by the mistakes they make but by the way they respond to those mistakes."

How are you responding to your past frustrations? Do you assume they merely foreshadow more anger, or do you look at your difficulties as opportunities to grow?

In Philippians 3:13–14 the apostle Paul (who had a history of disruptive anger) expressed an optimism that could be shared

> Forgetting those things which are behind and reaching forward to those things which are ahead, I press toward the goal for the prize of the upward call of God in Christ Jesus.
> —Philippians 3:13–14

by any Christian wishing to set aside old wounds: "Forgetting those things which are behind and reaching forward to those things which are ahead, I press toward the goal for the prize of the upward call of God in Christ Jesus." Paul was determined that his angry history would actually motivate him to change. This became his goal, and in his later years, his life exemplified kindness, compassion, servitude, assertiveness (not abrasiveness), and gentleness.

■ ■ ■ ■

If you traded your historical trends of anger for new goals, what would change in your lifestyle? *(For instance, rather than being disagreeable toward my opinionated brother-in-law, I would choose to initiate friendly conversations; instead of being known at work as a pessimist, I would maintain a reputation for encouragement.)*

1. _____

_____

2. _____

_____

3. _____

_____

■ ANCHOR YOURSELF IN TRUTH

During her counseling sessions, Cindy realized she had perpetuated her anger by allowing myths to guide her. By learning to challenge her own negative generalizations, she replaced the myths with truth. She came to recognize that while she had suffered she still had inner strength to draw upon.

Dr. Carter spoke with her about this. "Cindy, we both agree you have experienced unwanted problems. In light of those problems your frustration is normal and you shouldn't be expected to fake a cheery disposition. Simultaneously, I want you to realize that all your frustrations do not represent the ultimate truth."

"I know you're right," she said. "I've just got some old thinking habits that need to be adjusted."

"Think of this analogy. Suppose as a child you mislearned the definition of some vocabulary words and for a time you used these words in the wrong context. Later you realized your mistake as you discovered the correct definitions. You would be forced to do two things. First, you would have to recognize the wrong definitions and exchange them for the correct ones. Second, you would need to restructure your thoughts so you would speak the words correctly."

Cindy replied, "So you're suggesting my experiences have given me a false impression of real truth and I need to rearrange my way of thinking about things?"

"That's exactly what I'm suggesting. You can learn to interpret your world very differently."

Cindy's greatest accomplishment in counseling was to learn that she did not have to be imprisoned by false assumptions created by her past frustrations. While her thinking patterns would not change overnight, she knew her task was not impossible. Determined to manage anger properly, she chose not to live with negative generalizations.

6

:: Self-Inflicted Anger

■ Step 6. Keep your lifestyle habits consistent with your emotional composure.

When most people try to determine the reasons for their anger, they point to external pressures: My spouse is uncooperative. My parents neglected basic needs. My job is stressful. My finances are in shambles. My friends don't know how to relate to me. My children are rebellious. Problems like these certainly create anger, but they do not tell the whole story.

A lot of anger is due to self-inflicted wounds. Though the environment may in fact present difficulties, we all have free will to manage our adult lives. Some of us perpetuate our own anger by making poisonous choices. In chapter 1 we acknowledged that our world indeed can feel unfriendly or insensitive. It is interesting to note, though, that many of the people who complain loudest about their exposure to unfairness are their own worst enemies. For instance, a father may complain that politicians are stubborn and out of touch with the people, yet that same man may be stubborn and closed-minded with his own family members. Or perhaps a man states that he needs to become less agitated with his friends; but instead of developing habits that increase interpersonal sensitivities, he watches cage fighting television shows and spends hours playing violent video games. Likewise, a mother may rue the fact that she pops off too quickly toward her children, yet she won't miss an episode of reality TV depicting women backbiting and insulting each other. Similarly, a person may fill commute time in the car listening to talk radio that clearly encourages arguing and the expression of unbending opinions.

Do you grasp the theme here? It is easy to say, *Yes, life would be more enjoyable if I could be less angry,* yet we often hinder our own progress by making choices that fertilize the very anger we want to be rid of.

■ ■ ■ ■

What self-sabotaging choices do you make that perpetuate your inclination toward anger? *(For instance, I continue to socialize with people who bring out the worst in my priorities; I drink alcohol to excess, which keeps me from being my best.)*

1. _____

_____

2. _____

_____

3. _____

_____

■ ■ ■ ■

As you determine to contain your angry expressions and behaviors, be aware that the emotion does not arise out of a vacuum. Sure enough, the world around you can provide many reasons for you to feel tense and agitated; but since you cannot change what others say and do, your energies will be best spent examining the one person who can make a major difference in your quality of life. That person is *yourself*!

Steve sought help because of chronic fatigue and headaches. He had consulted many medical doctors, but each came to the same conclusion: "Medically you are sound, but emotionally you are your own worst enemy." His initial appointment at our clinic was with Dr. Minirth.

After hearing Steve describe his symptoms of physical sluggishness, Dr. Minirth asked him to talk about his emotional ups and downs. "How much time do we have?" Steve asked jokingly. "I've lived with one frustration after another for so long, I hardly know where to begin."

He recounted how his early family life had been reasonably good. "My dad was pretty strict and my mother just didn't understand me. But we didn't have any major problems. I was a pretty happy kid.

"My problems began about twenty years ago as I was becoming established in my career. I guess you could say I just didn't want to grow up. I had good jobs, but none ever lasted very long. I was only interested in wine, women, and song. I had quite a reputation as a free spirit."

"Did you marry?" Dr. Minirth asked.

"Yeah, I was married once for about ten months in my early twenties. But it was wrong from the start. I'm still not sure why I married the woman. A few years later I married again and it lasted about seven years. We got a divorce after my wife caught me fooling around. I can't blame her for wanting out. I know she wasn't happy. We had a boy who is now sixteen or seventeen. But they live in another state so I don't see them much." (It had been three years since he had seen his son.)

As they talked, Dr. Minirth came to agree that Steve was correct when he stated he did not want to grow up. He refused to take seriously any long-term responsibility. The result was financial strain, many broken relationships, moral bankruptcy, and spiritual emptiness.

Dr. Minirth told Steve, "You're here because you want to sort out the emotions related to your physical ailments, and I'm going to be very frank with you. My impression is that you've brought on most of your frustration yourself because you want to bend the rules to fit your momentary cravings. It will be hard to find stability until you make adjustments in some of these habits."

"I know you're right," Steve responded. "I've just got to decide if I really have the will power to adjust."

SABOTAGING EMOTIONAL STABILITY

Steve is not alone in bringing anger into his life through poor personal choices. You may not have the same hedonistic tendencies, but you may be able to relate to self-sabotage. In the following pages we will examine some of the more common ways this occurs.

Morals Decline

When we remember that anger is linked to the preservation of personal worth, needs, and convictions, it is safe to say frustrated people are searching for affirmation. When that affirmation is found through wholesome fellowship, anger is reduced. But too many people perpetuate their anger by compromising their morals to gain acceptance. In the short term, some satisfaction is felt. But over the long term immorality and emotional turmoil go hand in hand.

After initially consulting Dr. Minirth, Steve began intensive counseling with Dr. Carter. They discussed his symptoms and examined his personal history. In one of their early sessions Dr. Carter remarked, "Steve, you've come to our clinic because you know we are Christians. Yet I detect a lot of non-Christian philosophy in your lifestyle. You seem to be at odds with your beliefs."

> **Immorality and emotional turmoil go hand in hand.**

"Well, I do believe in God," Steve replied. "But my problem is that I want someone I can see and touch to tell me I'm OK. God is too abstract."

"So you've decided to place your hope in people. That's risky because they may not be on God's side."

"I know what you mean," Steve said, "and I can see how I have gotten myself in hot water because I have compromised my values. I guess I don't have the patience to trust God's guidance."

They discussed Steve's various episodes of moral decline. He regularly associated with the nightclub crowd. He had a history of promiscuity and pornography use. His social style was laced with frustrating relationships with unreliable peers. All of this gave him short-term thrills but long-term aggravation.

"Steve, one of your goals in counseling is reducing your anger and stress," said Dr. Carter. "It looks like your morality will be a good place for us to start. You're creating more frustration than you are eliminating."

How about you? Check the following statements that apply to you to help decide if morality problems play a role in your anger buildup.

☐ I cling to lustful thoughts and fantasies more often than I would like.

☐ I find myself skeptically questioning moral rules of living.

☐ There are times when I feel like two separate people, a public *good* person and a private *conniving* person.

☐ Going to church is more of a ritual than a truly purposeful experience.

☐ I am entertained by crude humor or sordid stories.

☐ I know that a more traditional manner of living would probably be good for me, but I hesitate to live that way.

☐ Short-term desires often override long-term wisdom.

☐ I am drawn toward entertainment that does not place a value on human dignity.

☐ There are people in my inner circle who entice me to turn my back on virtuous living.

☐ I have to struggle to maintain purity in my sexual habits.

☐ Cutting corners in my responsibilities is easier now than it was five years ago. I would rather spend a hedonistic night "out on the town" than a quiet evening at home.

☐ I have had several social relationships that began with a thrill but ended in frustration.

If you checked six or more of these statements, you can probably recall several times when anger occurred as the result of inevitable disillusionment.

Our modern, permissive world asks, "What does moral purity have to do with emotions?" Many assume that promiscuity or carousing is just plain fun. So why all the fuss?

Moral purity is more than a code of acceptable and unacceptable behavior. Ultimately morality is a reflection of our respect for others. It illustrates our belief in the dignity of human beings. For example, whenever a man or woman pursues someone with the intent of engaging in extramarital sex, some form of manipulation will be used. First impressions may create the appearance of care and friendliness, but because the behavior is void of a lasting commitment, it is, in truth, propelled by a "What's-in-it-for-me?" mind-set. Eventual rejection is a certainty. Human dignity is overlooked. Conversely, maintaining purity in sexuality represents a commitment to respectfulness and consideration.

The same could be said for a life of partying and general hedonism. For a while it can seem harmless and fun; but behind the scenes of this lifestyle is the question, *Who cares about human dignity?* As this continues, an unsettled feeling of emptiness can build inside the individual, and this eventually feeds emotional tension and restlessness.

A morally balanced life is anchored in purpose and meaning, and its primary focus is a loving, uplifting presence toward others. Immorality, however, gives people a sense of meaninglessness, since its primary focus is instant gratification at the expense of long-term contentment. This, then, begets the question, *Why am I so dissatisfied?* Frustration predictably emerges as the emptiness of immorality leaves people wandering through life with no overarching plan for inner peace.

Steve admitted to Dr. Carter, "Over the years there have been times when I have slowed down long enough to ponder who I am. I'm ashamed to say I sometimes feel disgusted with myself. But instead of incorporating a moral ethic, I inevitably go back to my carousing."

"I suspect your impatience keeps you from implementing more conservative values," said Dr. Carter. "At first it will feel awkward to tone down your wild ways. Yet moral purity can feel very rewarding as you enjoy the clean conscience it produces. You'll not regret it."

■ ■ ■ ■

What changes could you make in your lifestyle to reflect a greater appreciation for moral purity? *(For instance, I don't need to watch provocative movies because they only entice me to view pureness as an antiquated lifestyle.)*

1. _____

_____

_____

2. _____

_____

_____

3. _____

_____

_____

■ ■ ■ ■

Work Becomes All-Encompassing

Since Creation, work has been an integral part of human existence. The work of the first man, Adam, was keeping his garden and overseeing God's creation. This task was not given to Adam for negative reasons but for positive ones. God knew Adam would derive a feeling of purpose from assisting the Lord in maintaining his surroundings. We feel a healthy pride as we survey our accomplishments at the end of each day. We find intrinsic rewards when we busy ourselves with productive activities ranging from managing a household to performing manual labor to running a multimillion-dollar enterprise. Work is necessary for personal well-being.

Yet as fruitful as work can be, it is not life's ultimate aim. A retired surgeon once told Dr. Minirth, "I feel as if I have absolutely no usefulness anymore. I'm more frustrated now than ever." When they explored why, the man admitted, "I've given all my energies to being the finest surgeon I could be. I was proud of my reputation as the best in my field. But in the end, I've got to wonder if it was really worth it. I have no one I can call a true friend. My wife and I have nothing in common. We've got no hobbies. I guess I've been a one-dimensional person and now I'm paying the consequences."

This doctor felt angry because of a self-inflicted wound. He had made work his god. Relationships were a distant second on his priority list. Spiritual vigor was something he had intellectualized, but it was not real to him.

When people are consumed by work and busyness, they typically describe themselves as stressed. Stress has been used as such a vague, catchall term it deflects us from recognizing the anger that is a part of it. Overworked, stressful people are angry. They may not always shout and scream, but they nurse a growing sentiment that life lacks the zeal it should have. Personal needs are left wanting. The net result is the presence of traits that are associated with anger—easy annoyance, irritability, impatience, and the like.

■ ■ ■ ■

In your lifestyle, what indicates that work is robbing you of your joy? *(For instance, as a full-time parent, I overextend myself in trying to keep up with all my children's activities; even though I promise myself I'll leave the office early, I usually stay much later than I want.)*

1. _____

_____

2. _____

_____

■ ■ ■ ■

To remedy the frustrations created by excessive work, we need not go to the other extreme of excessive play. Balance *can* be achieved. Primarily, this occurs as relationships are nurtured and limits regarding activities are enforced. Notice the following examples that show a balance between work and stress reduction.

- A hardworking dad can take time out in the evening to play a board game with his children. This will remind him of the satisfaction found in family bonding.

- A harried mother can tell her children she is capable of driving them to a limited number of activities. They will have to choose which activities will receive her attention.

- An office worker can acknowledge that her world will not collapse if she regularly goes home at six o'clock. She will vow to resume her work as soon as she gets to her desk the next morning.

One workaholic sales representative complained to Dr. Minirth, "Your advice about limiting work sounds good in theory. But you are naive if you think a person in my position can really cut back on it."

"What you are saying," said Dr. Minirth, "is commonly expressed by people before they have a stroke or heart attack. It's amazing, though, how they change their tunes after open-heart surgery. I'm encouraging you to slow down now so your body won't give you the more drastic message a year or two from now."

The sales rep got the message.

■ ■ ■ ■

What about you? What evidence can you cite that you are finding balance between work and leisure? *(For instance, my household chores are completed during the week so the weekend can be devoted to family activities; I sometimes telephone a friend just to say hello rather than spending my evenings with my head buried in business magazines.)*

1. _____

_____

_____

2. _____

_____

_____

■ ■ ■ ■

Poor Health Habits Develop

"I hate my social life; it is so boring," said Cathy emphatically. "Everyone around me has lots going on, but I spend most weekends alone. No one seems to care!"

To hear Cathy's gripes you might assume she was the unfortunate victim of social isolation. But that wasn't her problem at all. Social opportunities were plentiful through church organizations and work contacts. But Cathy had an unkempt appearance and apparently had no plans to change any time soon. She was chronically overweight by about eighty-five pounds. She was angry because people thought of her as unattractive. Yet she brought on some of her problems herself by her careless abuse of her body.

Overeating is only one of the poor health habits related to self-inflicted anger. Others are also common: smoking, poor exercise, poor hygiene, lack of sleep. Each of these habits contributes to irritability or low self-esteem and reduces our quality of life. Such habits also cause us to focus on worries that might otherwise be avoided.

Cathy did not like the repercussions of her untidy appearance, but instead of taking responsibility for maintaining good habits, she chose to blame others for her problems. "Why is it you have to be a beauty queen to get attention?" she would ask. "Why won't anyone just accept me for what I am?"

"You have a valid point that acceptance should not be based on superficial criteria," Dr. Carter told her. "But I want you to be aware of a deeper issue that needs to be addressed. People look to you to tell them how they should feel about you. And when they notice that you seem to care little about your personal upkeep, they interpret that as an indication that you don't like yourself. So they respond in kind, perhaps subconsciously, to the message you send."

"So you're telling me the same thing my mother keeps saying, that I've got to go on a diet before anyone will like me. I really resent that!"

"I'm not telling you that you have to do anything," replied Dr. Carter. "How you care for yourself is your choice. I am simply saying you might resolve some of your anger by examining how you contribute to your own unwanted circumstances."

■ ■ ■ ■

What about you? Do you sometimes neglect your health to the point that it contributes to ongoing frustrations? What are some of your personal health concerns? (*For instance, my doctor tells me I have high blood pressure and I need to unwind with regular exercise, but I have yet to start on any program.*)

1. _____

_____

_____

2. _____

_____

_____

■ ■ ■ ■

Remember that one function of anger is standing up for perceived needs. You may be working against yourself by ignoring your needs and creating trouble. For example, overeaters may say they need a satisfying relationship, but when that doesn't happen, they turn to food for a temporary fix. Smokers may complain that they are tired of others' criticism, ignoring the annoying and unhealthy aspects of their smoking. Those who suffer ulcers or chronic headaches may bemoan their reduced ability to maintain full activities, while continuing to interact with their world in tense, controlling ways. In anger, they may demand that others cater to their needs, when they could eliminate that anger by caring for themselves more adequately.

■ ■ ■ ■

If you decided to take better care of your health, thus reducing your irritations, what adjustments would you make? *(For instance, instead of complaining about feeling out of shape, I will commit to an exercise program.)*

1. _____

_____

_____

2. _____

_____

_____

■ ■ ■ ■

Speaking to the Corinthian people who had many self-destructive habits, the apostle Paul instructed, "Glorify God in your body and in your spirit, which are God's" (1 Corinthians 6:20). This teaching has implications for our emotional healthiness because our physical health so strongly affects our feelings. People seeking to manage anger properly will correctly conclude that physical health is not an isolated factor but a powerful component of personal stability.

> Glorify God in your body and in your spirit, which are God's.
> —1 Corinthians 6:20

Material Gain Is Overemphasized

Speaking to Steve about the relationship between his priorities and his anger, Dr. Carter asked, "You've said you agree that a moral lifestyle is probably best, yet you've hesitated to commit to it. Why is that?"

"Well, to be honest, Doc, the conservative lifestyle seems too stodgy for me. I like to be where the action is. And I like nice things; I consider them the fruits of my labor."

"I share your preference for ongoing stimulation," replied Dr. Carter, "although I suspect we'd have different ideas of what that should be. But I get the feeling you equate stimulation with material gain. I'm assuming you like fancy cars, vacations, fine restaurants, things like that. Am I right?"

"Well, of course!" said Steve. "I mean, where's the fun if you're not getting ahead? I don't think God intends people to avoid the finer things in life. Do you?"

Dr. Carter explained, "If you can afford life's pleasures that's certainly nothing to be ashamed of. I draw the line, though, when material gain seems to be required for happiness."

Ultimately, emotional composure is derived from intangible elements. We reduce tension when we feel loved and respected, when we encourage others, and when understanding abounds. These things cannot be bought. They are decisions that reflect our spiritual vitality. In contrast, when we anchor our emotions to the false security of materialism, we make ourselves vulnerable to unnecessary forms of anger.

Perhaps the most common type of anger associated with material emphasis is envy, frustration over someone else's possession of something we want. If we win the race of materialism, we become vulnerable to false superiority. If we cannot acquire what we crave, we become vulnerable to discouragement.

Check the following statements that apply to you.

☐ I have a great desire to appear successful.

☐ I often put on a false front, hoping to create a good impression.

☐ I sometimes indulge fantasies of what it might be like "at the top."

☐ If I achieve something or buy something new, I want people to notice.

☐ I keep score of my own gains in comparison to the gains of friends and family.

☐ I feel frustrated because I haven't received the same lucky breaks as someone else.

☐ I spend too much money on things such as clothes or cars to the extent that I put myself in financial jeopardy.

☐ There have been times when I have passed along negative rumors about a successful person.

If you checked four or more statements, you are probably too dependent upon your material and social status for inner well-being.

■ ■ ■ ■

What are some specific indicators in your life of an overemphasis on material gain? *(For instance, when I shop, I charge whatever I want with the idea that I'll worry about paying for it later.)*

1. _____

_____

_____

2. _____

_____

_____

3. _____

_____

_____

■ ■ ■ ■

Not only does a material emphasis indicate a false foundation for security, it also puts us in an adversarial position toward others. Envious people are notoriously competitive, and often they see other individuals as objects of derision. If another person has more, he or she is the target of criticism about the way that gain was achieved. If a person has less, inner satisfaction is gained at that person's expense.

"Steve, I don't know if you've thought of your materialistic lifestyle as being pushed along by anger. But that's precisely what we're dealing with in your case," said Dr. Carter.

"I know there's a connection," Steve replied. "I'd like to know how to break it."

"First," suggested Dr. Carter, "let's acknowledge that you may not always feel frustrated at the moment you seek personal gain. For example, when you bought the car that was beyond your budget, you were probably smiling as you gave it a test drive. But subtle anger was lurking behind the scenes. I suspect your thoughts were something like, *I can't let people see me driving a piece of junk. I've got to find a way to make myself look better.*"

Steve reflected insightfully, "So you're saying I had a need for acceptance and I was frustrated at the prospect of not receiving it unless I was surrounded with the right trappings."

"That's exactly what I'm saying. So let me challenge you with a suggestion. Could you let go of your envious anger by acknowledging your legitimate needs, but realizing that material superiority and social climbing are not central to your fulfillment?"

"I know you're speaking sound ideas," said Steve. "But honestly, this will require some real inner adjustment."

■ ■ ■ ■

How about you? Respond to the following sentences:

More important to me than material gain is _____

_____

_____

To demonstrate that materialism does not have a grip on me I will

_____

_____

■ ■ ■ ■

Successful anger management involves standing firmly for personal needs. But to be balanced in seeking personal needs, we must first be certain they are truly needs. Most of our material needs are merely "wants." When needs and wants are kept in proper perspective, we will have decreased anger.

> When needs and wants are kept in proper perspective, we will have decreased anger.

Substance Abuse Is More Likely

In recent generations substance abuse has gained a foothold throughout the United States and much of the world. If you have school-age children, you have undoubtedly noticed how much more classroom instruction about drugs and alcohol your children receive compared with your own childhood education on these topics. Drug and alcohol awareness in our young people is good, in light of the temptations they face. But the fact that it is so necessary causes us to shudder at the shame of it all.

Young people's first experience with substance abuse is usually easy to explain by citing peer pressure. Wanting to feel valued by their peers, youths will cross the line of good moral judgment if they think they can get away with it. Their progression into substance-abusing adults also would be easy to explain by citing habit or just plain pleasure.

But more is involved in substance abuse than just peer pressure or habit or pleasure. Ultimately, it is an act of anger that creates susceptibility to more anger. Think of it this way: When a person first drinks alcohol or uses an illicit drug, invariably an inner thought says, *I really shouldn't be doing this.* But another, more rebellious thought eventually occurs: *Go on, do it. Just make sure you don't get caught.* Most of us would agree that the initial acts of substance abuse are rebellious in nature. Now think further. What emotion is most closely linked to rebellion? Anger.

Through their behavior, substance abusers are communicating, *I have my needs, and I want to feel respected.* These can be elements of legitimate anger, as described in Chapter 1. But this means of satisfying those needs is irresponsible. In some way it causes people—the abusers and those associated with them—to be hurt. Anger is then perpetuated through the inevitable strained relationships.

Dr. Carter spoke with Steve about the effects of substance abuse in his major relationships. "Apparently the party scene has been very important to you throughout your adult life. Sidestepping the morality issues for a moment, I'd like to explore how this has affected your closest relationships."

"Well, my problem is that I haven't kept up very well with my family," Steve said. "I guess they've become less important to me. I stay in touch with my parents to some extent; they're retired now. But we don't get together more than a couple of times each year. And my son lives out of state with his mother. He's in high school and doesn't have much time for me."

"That must make you feel frustrated, knowing you have such little rapport with the ones you love."

"I'd feel frustrated if I let myself think about it," Steve replied. "But I just go my own way and let others worry about those things."

Keep in mind that Steve's original symptoms were fatigue, headaches, and lack of motivation, all signals of emotional exhaustion. How did his substance abuse contribute to his emotional duress? It allowed him to tend to his perceived needs, but at the expense of family stability. Ultimately, this became a self-defeating way of life. But because his substance abuse was his way of hiding his anger behind a feel-good mask, his emotions were stored away until he became so weary of his lifestyle that he physically collapsed in futility.

■ ■ ■ ▢

How about you? Have you ever abused alcohol or other substances? What were you hiding from? *(For instance, using alcohol let me temporarily escape from the pain in my marriage.)*

1. _____

_____

_____

2. _____

_____

_____

Although substance abuse allows you to escape your problems temporarily, it usually increases ill will in your closest relationships. If you have this problem, what ill effects can be traced to your substance abuse? *(For instance, my spouse and I seem to have more arguments than ever.)*

1. _____

_____

_____

2. _____

_____

_____

■ ■ ■ ▢

An alternative to substance abuse is open, constructive communication about personal needs. Rather than hiding from the grind of exploring emotions, you can commit yourself to ongoing problem-solving efforts.

■ ■ ■ ■

How might this commitment impact your relationship habits? *(For instance, rather than unwinding from my job stress by having a few drinks, I could work with my coworkers to implement ongoing dialogues for problem-solving purposes.)*

1. _____

_____

2. _____

_____

■ ■ ■ ■

Spiritual Life Is Ignored

Anger management is ultimately linked to spiritual stability. When we maintain a daily relationship with God, our problems are less overwhelming. When we maintain a sense of worth in God, we are less susceptible to irritability if others are rejecting or noncommunicative or rude. Being at peace with God empowers us to confidently combat worldly imperfections.

But when a spiritual vitality is absent, personal stability is no longer a matter of inner strength. Instead, it is linked more than ever to people and circumstances. This creates great vulnerability to anger, because people and circumstances are fickle.

Of all the subjects discussed with Dr. Carter, Steve struggled most with his spiritual life. "I went to Sunday school as a boy, so I know right from wrong. But I've gotten out of the habit of attending church, and I never read the Bible or talk to people about God. Religion just isn't a part of my life anymore."

"Look what you've replaced it with," said Dr. Carter, "and then reflect on how that influences your emotions."

"I haven't really thought about it that way, but I suppose I've replaced religion with pleasure. Usually when I'm in the middle of a pleasant activity, my emotions are great. But in the aftermath my emotions are empty."

"Steve, if you're like most people your carousing spirit feeds a calloused feeling toward people. You become so tuned into your own desires that the needs of others become insignificant. In the long run this creates anger, because no one is there when you really need a friend."

Steve began crying. "I've alienated myself from my family. The only people I'm close to are my party buddies. But they have the same emptiness I have. It creates a cycle of unending frustration," he said.

■ ■ ■ ■

What signs in your life indicate a depletion of your spiritual life? *(For instance, I no longer enjoy worship services; worldly fun is more and more enticing to me than ever.)*

1. _____

   _____

2. _____

   _____

How does your lack of spiritual strength create frustration? *(For instance, I've found that my nonspiritual friends encourage me to do whatever I want, but that behavior alienates me from my family.)*

1. _____

   _____

   _____

2. _____

   _____

   _____

■ ■ ■ ■

Developing your spiritual life involves more than attending church regularly. It starts with a recognition that relying on God for meaning in life is both essential and desirable. It then follows that you will seek out God's will by exploring Scripture and committing your lifestyle to His direction. Finally, it involves being regularly associated with people of a similar persuasion, giving and receiving strength in godly relationships.

■ ■ ■ ■

As you seek to deepen your spiritual well-being, what adjustments could you make? *(For instance, I would like to become involved in ongoing classes that teach the pertinence of biblical truth.)*

1. _____

   _____

   _____

2. _____

   _____

   _____

■ WHERE TO GO FROM HERE

In this and the three preceding chapters, we have examined how learned patterns of relating, thinking, and behaving influence anger. As you succeed in adjusting these patterns you will experience increased composure.

But there are other emotional problems that can also perpetuate anger when they are left unresolved. Our emotions closely affect one another, so when one emotion remains unresolved, we continue to be vulnerable to anger. In the next chapters we will explore how a propensity toward anger can be created by four major emotions: pride, fear, loneliness, and inferiority.

Part Three

How Other Emotions Create Anger

7

How Pride Influences Anger

■ **Step 7. Live in humility rather than self-preoccupied pride.**

It was past supper time when Ken walked through his back door. His wife Tina shouted from the den, "I'm in here, Honey. Come on back!"

As he stepped into the room Tina could see that Ken was in no mood for fun and games. He looked tired. "I'll bet you're hungry. Looks like you could use something to eat. If you give me fifteen minutes I can heat some supper for you."

Ken exploded. "You knew what time I'd be home! Why couldn't you have something ready for me now? Don't you ever think about anyone besides yourself?" he shouted.

"I'm sorry, Honey. I just didn't want to get something prepared and then take the chance that it would be cold by the time you came in. Just go change clothes, and I'll have everything ready as quickly as I can."

On his way to the bedroom, Ken stopped by his daughters' room where his two grade-school-age girls were fussing. Agitated, he griped at them, "What's the deal with you two? Can't you get along for just one day? If you don't cut out this bickering right now, you'll be sorry. I don't need any of this!"

Ken eventually washed his face, changed clothes, parked behind the newspaper at the kitchen table and ate his meal in stony silence. For the rest of the evening Tina and the two girls stayed out of his way. They had seen Ken in this foul mood many times before. They knew if anything or anyone pushed him he could fly into an ugly rage.

Sitting in Dr. Carter's office, Tina explained, "I'm very weary of living in such a tense home. Ken's anger is beyond description. The most minor setbacks cause him to erupt. I'm constantly wondering when he will go into one of his tirades. Something's got to give or I'm leaving the marriage."

"Oh, you've threatened that so many times it doesn't even register with me anymore," Ken responded. "I live a stressful life and sometimes I blow off some steam. Do you think I'm the only person who's ever raised his voice a few times? Why don't you quit feeling so sorry for yourself?"

Tina turned toward Dr. Carter. "I'm at my wit's end. I don't think I'm an irresponsible wife. Ken will tell you that I'm good to him and I'm reliable. But his anger is so overpowering it's wearing me down."

Speaking to Ken, Dr. Carter asked, "Do you feel there's a problem with your anger?"

"Yeah, I guess. I mean, I wouldn't be here if everything was great. So I know there are problems. Maybe I should ease up on my frustrations; but don't expect me to take the blame for everything that's wrong in our family."

During their initial session Ken decided he needed help in understanding the meaning of his rages. So he agreed to some individual discussions with Dr. Carter to get to the root of his problems. In the first few sessions they discussed how much of his anger was a cover for insecurity. He said his father had been very harsh and he had little feeling of true affirmation from his peers. Early in life he learned to brush off his relational emptiness by claiming how unimportant affirmation was to him. But during his counseling sessions Ken admitted he really did feel a craving to be loved.

Ken and Dr. Carter explored Ken's history of control. Having been exposed to powerful controls as a boy, he had determined that no one would ever control him again. Yet he had carried this determination too far by developing in himself the very overpowering habits he disliked so much in others.

Insights like these helped Ken gain a better comprehension of his anger, so in the first few weeks of counseling he experienced some success in tempering his explosiveness.

But one Thursday morning Ken bluntly told Dr. Carter, "I don't know if I'm ever going to get a grip on my anger. How can I when Tina won't pay attention to me? And my girls . . . they see that Mom doesn't treat me right so they give me no respect either. Last night I had another one of my rages and let them know I'd better be given the proper respect or we were going to have an all-out war."

Dr. Carter remarked, "Ken, we've discussed before that standing up for self-respect can be legitimate. But something's going on in your personality that needs to be exposed. You seem consumed with yourself. A high percentage of your rages occur when you aren't receiving what you want."

We then began to discuss how Ken's anger was propelled by pride, the emotion of self-absorption. At times his ego seemed so large that he could focus on nothing but his momentary desires. He is not unlike any of the rest of us, at least to the extent that we all struggle with this trait.

WHAT IS PRIDE?

From the beginning of life we are preoccupied with ourselves. Although you probably cannot remember your toddler years, you know how this trait exhibited itself then. You cried when a parent told you no. You grabbed your favorite toy if another child wanted to play with it. You refused to eat if you were not given the food you preferred. You ignored your parents when they attempted to give you directions.

We chuckle as we reflect on how we must have acted in those very early years. Young children are excused for such antics because they don't know any better. But consider how self-preoccupation continues as the personality develops. Each year this characteristic is less blatant, but it can still dominate. Rather than manifesting itself in the same way it does in a whiny toddler, self-preoccupation in adults becomes pride that nonetheless maintains a foothold in our attitudes. As a result we continue to exhibit insensitivities and callousness. We can be certain any episode of unhealthy anger is tainted by this trait.

■ ■ ■ ■

We often limit our understanding of pride by thinking of it in narrow terms. When you think of a proud person, what mental impression do you hold? *(For instance, I think of someone who is very boastful or arrogant.)*

_____

_____

_____

■ ■ ■ ■

To understand how pervasive pride is, you will need to set aside stereotyped ideas and stretch your mind to include a very broad spectrum of behaviors. Pride is more than just arrogance or conceit. It is at the core of virtually any unhealthy, nonproductive emotion or behavior. Specifically, it plays a very influential role in problems with anger.

> Pride is more than just arrogance or conceit. It is at the core of virtually any unhealthy, nonproductive emotion or behavior.

To determine how you struggle with pride, check the following statements that apply to you. As you go through this checklist, see if you can identify the self-absorption inherent in each item.

☐ I tend to speculate why people are not as considerate as I think they should be.

☐ When someone is insensitive, I let it bother me more than it really should.

☐ Impatience or edginess overcomes me when people act incompetently.

☐ Sometimes I fantasize what life would be like if I could have ideal circumstances.

☐ My moods tend to rise and fall, depending on how others show me respect.

☐ When I express my opinions, I am disgruntled if the other person does not receive them well.

☐ I am known for having a strong personality.

☐ When I witness something good in another person's life, my initial reaction is to wish for the same thing in my life.

☐ In social circles I feel the need to keep an unblemished reputation, even if it requires a cover-up.

☐ I would prefer to avoid disclosures of a personal nature.

If you checked five or more items, your pride has gained a foothold on your emotions. Anger is inevitable.

Pride Is Our Spiritual Disease

To understand the influence pride can have on personality, it is important to recognize how it is intricately linked to our inborn sinfulness. Pride is a spiritual disease that is the manifestation of our innate sinful nature. In Chapter 4 we mentioned how God had given Adam (who represents each of us) the instruction to be free

> Pride is a spiritual disease that is the manifestation of our innate sinful nature.

while refraining from the temptation to be Godlike in applying knowledge. But in choosing to defy God's command, Adam took control of his own life. The inner push that prompted him to do this was his pride. In tempting Adam, Satan succeeded in encouraging him to develop a self-preoccupied pattern of thinking. *I've got a good mind,* Adam reasoned, in effect. *Why shouldn't I try to order the world to fit my mold?*

Once Adam succumbed to this self-preoccupied thinking, it became an integral part of his personality. A day could not pass without many self-absorbed thoughts. That tendency was then embedded in successive generations. The Bible refers to this as being "in Adam." Even today, it is apparent in the youngest child and the oldest adult. We cannot rid ourselves of it.

This inborn sinful nature accompanies all inappropriate forms of anger. Whether we shout or ridicule or criticize or withdraw in abusive silence, we nurse the thought, *Why can't people be what I say they should be?* Even when we plan to be gracious in our emotions, those plans falter quickly if events run counter to our preferences. This tendency caused the apostle Paul to confess, "For what I will to do, that I do not practice; but what I hate, that I do" (Romans 7:15).

No amount of psychotherapy can completely rid us of pride, no more than we can totally eliminate a problem such as our vulnerability to disease or unwanted aches and pains. We can learn to minimize its effects, but it will plague us as long as we live on this side of heaven.

■ ■ ■ ■

Can you think of a recent incident that illustrates how a toddler can reveal his or her chronic self-preoccupation? *(For instance, when my grandson wants to play a game, he will pitch a fit if someone doesn't respond right away.)*

1. _____

_____

_____

2. _____

_____

_____

Because self-preoccupation is central to our sinful nature, it can be found in our adult problems too. What are your most common struggles that manifest this trait? *(For instance, my impatience is easily aroused; I become sullen and moody when someone speaks ill of me.)*

1. _____

_____

2. _____

_____

3. _____

_____

4. _____

_____

■ ■ ■ ■

Ken sat quietly for a moment after he and Dr. Carter identified the extent of his self-preoccupied tendency. Then, very thoughtfully, he spoke. "I've heard ministers say pride precedes our falls. And I've admitted that when I am demanding, it is my pride at work. But I never realized it was as widespread as this. It's everywhere in my personality."

"While anger is not the only way pride is revealed," said Dr. Carter, "you can get a good idea of how strong your pride is by recognizing how anger reflects self-preoccupation. Whether it's open aggression or passive aggression, your mind is focused on you, your rights, and your preferences."

Trying to grasp the concept clearly, Ken commented, "When you say pride is part of our inborn sinful nature, you seem to imply that I cannot blame anyone else for its presence in my life. I'm fully responsible for it."

"You're so right," said Dr. Carter. "I'm glad to hear you make that connection because it will help you temper your anger. You've been insisting that Tina or the girls are the cause of your anger. That leads to the false conclusion that your anger will go away if you can force them to act as you want them to act. But by saying your anger is a manifestation of your sinfulness, we can conclude that your anger can be managed only as you come to proper terms with God."

"Any other time people have told me to get right with God, I just brushed it off as a preachy cliché," said Ken. "But the way you have explained it makes sense. I know this self-preoccupation has been within me since my earliest memories, so it really is unfair to expect my family to cater to me and somehow relieve me of my frustrations." Ken was making a major breakthrough in understanding his anger.

▨ CHOOSING HUMILITY

Because pride is so closely linked to our sinful spiritual condition, its resolution hinges on finding a healthier spiritual alternative. Repeatedly, New Testament instructions urge us to deny self, letting God be God. Paradoxically, as we set aside our preoccupation with our own personal needs, our need for real peace is met. Peace emanates from submission to God's authority, not in demanding our own way.

■ ■ ▨ ▨

When you consider the concept of denying self, what struggles could this potentially cause? *(For instance, I'm afraid if I deny myself I'd be everyone's doormat.)*

_____

_____

_____

■ ■ ▨ ▨

While denying self may appear to be a weakness, it actually clears the way for unusual strength. Rather than pridefully wondering how you can make people do as you wish, self-denial can prompt you to ponder how to please God in your activities. Because God's plan always leads to healthy interaction, we are assured that this submission will bring us more successes than failures.

The trait that keeps us in submission to God is humility. The opposite of pride, submission is a *lack* of self-preoccupation and a willingness to acknowledge personal limits. Ken, for example, had to recognize that his wife and daughters were not obligated to cater to his every whim. He needed to admit he was limited in his ability to force his preferences on them. He was not the center of the universe. He had pluses and minuses just like everyone else. So his "treat-me-as-king" mentality was ill advised.

Dr. Carter told him, "Ken, it sounds strange, but positive transformation can come only after you admit that you have no right to expect godlike adoration from anyone."

"It's hard to argue against your words," he responded. "I guess I'm going to have to get used to the idea that humility is a strength."

"I consider Christ to be the ultimate model of strength," said Dr. Carter, "and Scripture indicates that humility was the cornerstone of His personality. He could speak forcefully, but He was constantly a submissive representative of God."

Then Ken and Dr. Carter discussed some common examples of how humility could be demonstrated in Ken's life.

- When his daughters fussed, rather than griping about the inconvenience it caused he could first remind himself that all children, even his own, are imperfect.

- When voicing his opinions or setting boundaries, he could do so without condescension.

- He would acknowledge that Tina had an identity separate from him; she did not live just to meet his needs.

- Rather than demanding that he should be served, he could look for ways to be a servant.

- By establishing a reputation as a listener, a friendlier atmosphere could develop in his home.

- Rather than sulking when things did not go well, he could remember that the world owes him nothing.

■ ■ ■ ■

How about you? What changes would you make if humility was more firmly established in your lifestyle? *(For instance, I'd quit worrying about what my friends think of me; I'd be more willing to admit when I'm wrong.)*

1. _____

_____

_____

2. _____

_____

_____

3. _____

  _____

  _____

■ ■ ■ ■

Let's look at some of the characteristics of humility and the ways it can be incorporated into our personalities.

Humility Is Other-Focused

As the emotion of self-preoccupation, pride's bottom line is, *Get my needs met.* Meeting needs is not always wrong, of course, but it can become such an all-consuming drive that a person becomes obsessed about how others can and should respond to him or her. When we worry too much about the effect of others' behavior on our lives, we respond too sensitively when a need is ignored or when other people have a focus that is different from ours.

Ken admitted this tendency affected him frequently. "I guess I'm at my worst when I get home from work. I'm weary because of the constant demands on me from customers. So I figure it's my turn for a little kindness. But I often forget that my family may have had a rough day too."

Dr. Carter replied, "It's easy to be so focused on your immediate needs that you put the family's needs completely out of your mind. Is this the only place you do this?"

"No. To be honest, I'm pretty demanding with my coworkers too. We sell computer software, so good service is a must. Sometimes I am so demanding about how my fellow employees treat customers that I forget they are humans with real feelings."

■ ■ ■ ■

When do you become so focused on getting your needs met that you step on others' feelings? (*For instance, I am so concerned about peace and quiet that when I discipline my daughter I have little regard for her feelings.*)

1. _____

   _____

   _____

2. _____

   _____

   _____

■ ■ ■ ■

A crucial biblical instruction for successful relating is to consider others more important than yourself. We are so naturally selfish we must consciously tune in to others. This requires us to be sensitive to others' feelings and to recognize that their differing perceptions can have full validity. Some examples of this quality follow.

> A crucial biblical instruction for successful relating is to consider others more important than yourself.

- Although you are engrossed in a project at work, you can take time to notice how a coworker's day is going and do something simple (like paying a compliment) to brighten his or her day.

- When you are preparing to have guests in your home, you can ease your perfectionistic requirements and focus instead on creating a relaxed, frustration-free atmosphere.

- When a friend tells you something personal, you can make a mental note of it and ask a follow-up question the next time you are together.

- When your mate tells you about something that happened earlier in the day, instead of immediately responding with a story about your day, you could ask a few follow-up questions first.

- Rather than telling a family member what he or she ought to do to make your home run more smoothly, you can set an example worthy of imitation.

As Ken pondered this idea of being sensitive to others, he protested, "When I was a boy I was trained to always consider how my behavior affected others. And honestly, it got old. I was weary of having to always worry about how everyone else felt. It's a type of imprisonment."

"I'm not suggesting that you be held hostage to others' preferences," said Dr. Carter. "In fact, if you tune in to others only because it is the dutiful thing to do, they'll catch on quickly and it will produce a negative effect. I am suggesting that you compare your emotional disposition when you're self-focused to your disposition when you are being genuinely kind. As the saying goes, kindness is its own reward. Others benefit and you feel clean."

"You're breaking my behavior down into a black-or-white choice," said Ken.

"In a sense I guess I am. You can choose to be self-focused; but be prepared for angry consequences. Or you can choose to be sensitive to others. Then you can be prepared for greater cohesion in your relationships. I'm hoping you'll see that sensitivity is a desirable choice rather than something you have to do."

■ ■ ■ ▪

If you chose to exchange self-focus for increased sensitivity, what would change in your lifestyle? *(For instance, I'd watch less TV and talk more openly with my wife about things that matter to her.)*

1. _____

_____

_____

2. _____

_____

_____

3. _____

_____

_____

HUMILITY ACCEPTS LIMITS

To establish patterns of successful assertiveness, boundaries must be recognized. First, we must establish personal boundaries, including anything from communicating simple needs to standing openly for deep convictions. Second, we must accept others' differentness. This requires us to refrain from being petty or overbearing as we communicate our needs and convictions.

Prideful persons struggle to maintain balance in such boundaries. They tend to communicate their needs and convictions with the assumption that no one could possibly disagree with them. They are imposing or easily offended. Also, they do not like to accept unique distinctions in others. In this sense, they are quite critical.

Consider the following examples of how pride keeps us from respecting good boundaries:

- A mother insists that her daughter should dress precisely as she wants her to. She becomes angry and argumentative when the daughter expresses her own preferences.

- A husband knows how his wife should feel about his extended family, and he is offended when she fails to show them the affection he expects.

- A sales representative does not like his supervisor's provisions for accountability, and he wants to work within his own guidelines.

- Listening to a woman talk about how she cannot live much longer in her current marriage, a friend quotes Bible passages, insisting that the woman handle the problem the friend's way.

Remember that Adam's first prideful act was to eat fruit from the forbidden tree in an attempt to be like God. Within each of us is that same desire to have a Godlike ability to shape the world in the way we want. We do not like to think of ourselves as limited. We know how the world should be, and this causes us to overlook our human limitations, trying instead to be kings and queens.

How does the inability to accept limits create anger? We are guaranteed to fail in our God-mimicking efforts, and this ensures frustration. No matter how brilliant we think we are or how persuasive we can be, we are totally and completely incapable of being gods. By attempting to push our preferences and ideas on to others, we create turmoil. As an analogy, think of the tension you would feel if you were given the assignment of composing an entire symphony in one day. Most of us wouldn't even know where to begin! The assignment would be so far beyond our human capacity we would be guaranteed dismal failure. So it is when we refuse to accept our boundaries. It is impossible. We are that limited.

■ ■ ■ ■

In what ways do you fail to accept your personal limits? *(For instance, I keep trying to reshape my spouse so he is more to my liking, but I just can't convince him of how he should change.)*

1. _____

_____

_____

2. _____

_____

_____

■ ■ ■ ■

Anger management requires us to willingly recognize our personal limits. When we become responsibly assertive, we relinquish the dream that the world can and should fit our personal preferences. As we build a foundation of stability, we accept pain and imperfection.

Check the following statements that apply to you.

☐ I can handle the fact that many people (even my closest family members) will differ from me in preference and opinion.

☐ When someone errs, it is not my position to criticize or judge.

☐ I refrain from giving advice or suggestions when I know they won't be appreciated anyway.

☐ As I speak my needs, I am aware that others are under no requirement to oblige me.

☐ I accept the fact that pain will exist in my life, and no amount of wishing can make it go away completely.

☐ I can endorse the variety of feelings and inclinations that exist within healthy relationships, including my closest relationships.

The more of these statements you agree with, the more you will be capable of living within realistic limits.

■ ■ ■ ■

As you consider how personal limits affect your anger, what adjustments could you make in your behavior? (*For instance, I could allow my teenager to express his individuality more openly.*)

1. _____

_____

_____

2. _____

_____

_____

■ ■ ■ ■

As Ken discussed the acceptance of personal limits with Dr. Carter, he said, "This one is going to be hard for me. When I was a boy I felt that limits were too strictly enforced. So as a man I have resisted being tied down by anyone."

"There is a major difference in the type of limits we are discussing now and the limits you had as a child," said Dr. Carter. "Back then, restrictions were imposed on you whether you liked it or not; free will was not really a factor. Now, however, we begin with the assumption that if you really insist on it, you can attempt to live as if there are no limits. We'll allow free will to play a pivotal role in your decisions. I'm assuming, though, that you would soon realize a no-limits life is not realistic. Instead, I suggest you accept limitations because they are simply a part of who you are."

Ken realized this acceptance would lead to some changes, both obvious and subtle. One obvious change was reducing his harshness at home, allowing his wife and children to be freer in their preferences and encouraging them to talk honestly about family decisions. The subtle changes included being less persuasive in his tone of voice and more tolerant as others spoke enthusiastically about subjects he cared little about.

Does Humility Require Suppressing Emotions?

At one of our seminars a woman asked, "If I set aside my pride in favor of humility, doesn't that mean I lose a large portion of myself? I mean, wouldn't I have to repress a lot of my real feelings?"

We responded, "If you practice humility only as an act of duty, it would indeed cause repressed emotions. But then, it wouldn't *really* be humility. You'd be living in legalism, which can be a subtle form of pride."

True humility does not require any false manipulation of the emotions. Humility is not an obligation or a duty. It is a choice. Recognizing it as a choice, we can decide to accept humility by first acknowledging that we can be wildly angry. We can scream. We can be passively aggressive. No one can take those options away. But the further we proceed in sifting through our choices, the more common sense shows us humility is a preferred option to unhealthy anger because it brings healthier consequences. By accepting our limits and setting aside self-preoccupations, we are not repressing the other emotions. We are putting a higher priority on appropriateness.

As Ken discussed the implications of humility with Dr. Carter, he reflected, "It is going to take time to get used to this pattern of thinking. I'm going to feel awkward as I try to remind myself that Tina and the girls should be given priority over my own wishes."

"Ken, I don't want you to make this choice because I gave you a good sales talk about it. I want your adjustments to be truly internally motivated."

"But how does that happen?" he asked.

"Remind yourself that if you really want to, you can remain in your self-preoccupied state. No one can force you to change if you really don't want to do it."

"But I'm getting tired of the emotional garbage that lies in the wake of my selfishness. I don't like it."

"I was hoping you would draw that conclusion," said Dr. Carter. "If you truly choose humility, then do it without denying your strong emotions. Instead, let it be the desire of your heart."

Once we accept our humble limitations, our propensity to inner anger will change. For example:

- When we speak assertively, it will be with the understanding that others still may opt to disagree.

- Once it becomes clear some ongoing imperfections will remain in our lives, we can choose to drop the anger and accept our circumstances for what they are.

- We can commit to lifelong improvement while realizing we will never have a problem-free life.

- We will see our unhealthy anger for what it is, self-destructive and harmful to others.

■ ■ ■ ■

How about you? What could you change in your relationships by acknowledging that humility is not a duty but a choice? *(For instance, I would recognize that I could continue to criticize my husband, but instead I will choose to give him compliments, knowing we all lose when I act condescendingly.)*

1. _____

_____

_____

2. _____

_____

_____

■ ■ ■ ■

Learning to let go of undesirable emotions rather than repressing them is unnatural to many. If you have had a history of abuse or if you are accustomed to being invalidated, you have probably learned well the trait of repression. To develop humility without repression will require ongoing self-examination: *Do I really mean it when I act kindly? Are there unspoken needs I should still address? When I claim to forgive, am I doing it on my own initiative?*

Remember, your effort will be lifelong. Just when you think you have mastered pride, it will reappear. Your commitment to humility needs to be repeated daily.

8

:: Fear's Effect on Anger

■ **Step 8. Hold your defenses to a minimum; trust your healthy assertions.**

With a stony expression, Diane sat in Dr. Minirth's office, explaining why she sought counseling. "No one has ever really appreciated me. My father was abrasive, and my mother was too caught up in her own neuroses to notice me," she said. "I've just about given up hope of ever having a satisfying relationship with a man, but really, I don't even care about that any more. You can't be open with men anyway. They're too unpredictable. Some of them pretend to love you, but it's just an illusion."

At age thirty-nine Diane was a prisoner of anger. She had never married and had few real friends. Her career as a legal secretary provided sufficient self-reliance. Yet she was not really pleased with her workplace. "Too many egos in one place," she would say. Diane told Dr. Minirth she wanted to be rid of her many resentments, but in the next sentence she said she was uncertain she could let go of them. "What do I have to look forward to?" she asked.

"I'd like to hear more about your personal history," said Dr. Minirth. "Current problems often have deep roots. What is your earliest memory of this pessimism?"

"On a scale of one to ten, my father was an eleven as tyrants go. He ruled with an iron fist. I learned very early not to cross him because I'd have misery for days if I did. He could go into a tirade at the drop of a hat. Nothing ever pleased him, so I just stayed out of his way."

"But in the meantime," reflected Dr. Minirth, "your emotions piled up inside."

"Oh, absolutely; but no one knew. My older brother, though, was a different story. He'd get into arguments with Dad almost daily. Friction between the two of them was terrible. There was constant chaos and misery."

"And your mother? Where was she while all this was going on?"

"Dr. Minirth, I really felt pity for my mom," said Diane. "She was the ultimate worrywart, always fretting about something. She'd get easily pulled into the family fracas, then my dad or brother would reduce her to tears. I never felt I could talk to her because she was always so uptight. She was home a lot, so at least she took care of my basic needs. But she was too burdened to really know me."

"How has this history affected your adult life?" Dr. Minirth continued.

"I've always been hungry for close friends," she replied, "but no one ever seems to be there when I need someone the most. I went out socially with some girlfriends in my twenties and thirties, but we weren't really tight, if you know what I mean. Also, I've tried to date occasionally, but it seems like there's an invisible barrier that pops up when I start to get to know a man. I'm not sure what the problem is, but guys just don't last long with me."

"I tried online dating and it was a disaster. Guys are interested in only one thing, and I'm amazed at how forward they can be when they let you know what a woman is supposed to do to prop up their egos. I've quit using the other online communities, too, because they are so fake. Besides, you never know if someone is just lurking out there, trying to find ways to manipulate you."

"And you're discouraged because you're almost forty, still single, and not sure who you can trust?" asked Dr. Minirth.

"Well, yeah, I guess so. After being single this long you get used to it, but it isn't what I had expected."

Dr. Minirth wanted to help Diane identify the elements beneath her anger, so he probed, "When you try to comprehend the reasons for your anger, what do you come up with?"

"I know I have a hard time trusting people," she said. "It becomes a never-ending cycle. I want to get close to someone, but I'm sure I send signals indicating discomfort. So that person rejects me, and I get mad. Then when another potential relationship comes along, I'm all the more skeptical; so the cycle repeats itself."

> Fear sets the stage for many dysfunctional behaviors and attitudes.

"I'm hearing you say you are guided by your fears," said Dr. Minirth.

"Fear? I always knew I was angry, but I didn't think I was living in fear."

Diane was making the common mistake of stereotyping fear. She was not overtly fretful, as her mother was. She didn't have any major phobias; nor was she prone to anxiety attacks. So it was easy for her to assume she did not have fears. Insecurities yes. But fears?

IDENTIFYING FEAR

Fear implies hesitancy, apprehension, and doubt. It is an emotional governor that inhibits us from living with full-throttle confidence. It sets the stage for many dysfunctional behaviors and attitudes. But it does not always have the image we expect.

■ ■ ■ ■

When you think of a fearful person, what mental image is most typical? (*For instance, I think of someone who is very unassertive and cowardly.*)

_____

_____

■ ■ ■ ■

Most of us identify fear in overtly weak characteristics such as shyness or cowering or intimidation. Certainly, those qualities have strong elements of fear. But fear is not one-dimensional. It can be expressed by unrealistic bravado, excessive talking, workaholism, and lying, to name a few traits. Fear is the inner insecurity that inhibits us from living in the healthy ways we know we should.

To get an idea of the ways fear may exist in your life, check the following statements that apply to you.

- ☐ I feel antsy or uncomfortable when I am not in control of things.
- ☐ I have been told I don't receive others' feedback well.
- ☐ There are parts of my personality no one knows about.
- ☐ Too often I feel the need to justify or rationalize my decisions.
- ☐ People don't know me as well as they might think they do.
- ☐ Sharing intimate feelings or personal thoughts with others is not natural for me.
- ☐ Sometimes I use humor to avoid delicate subjects, or I change topics quickly.
- ☐ The moods of other people can have a strong effect on my moods.
- ☐ I have a habit of letting my frustrations fester inwardly; I don't let go of them easily.
- ☐ I have been known to tell lies to cover up flaws or to keep from being accountable.
- ☐ When someone is clearly angry, I habitually seek to "cover my flank."
- ☐ I worry more about my public image than most people would suspect.

Each of the above statements represents a subtle form of fear. If you checked six or more, you probably struggle too often with this emotion and in turn you bring frustration and anger into your world.

FEAR CAUSES DEFENSIVENESS

Fear is revealed in cover-ups and phoniness. It keeps us from being fully honest about who we are, prompting us instead to project false or only partially true images of ourselves. Fearful individuals have learned to be cautious in self-revelation, prompting evasiveness or edginess. Perhaps the most reliable way to identify fear is by defensiveness.

Three Categories of Defense

Defensiveness includes any resistance tactic intended to shield ourselves from perceived threats. Realistically, it is normal to have some defenses because our world inevitably presents threatening situations. But too often we overuse our defenses, indicating unresolved fears.

Three distinct categories of defense occur most commonly in personal relations: denial, evasiveness, and reversal. Let's examine each one.

Denial is a refusal to acknowledge personal problems or tensions. In most cases denial is subconscious; avoiding issues is so central to the person's character it occurs without overt deliberation. It is as though there is a need to exist beyond humanness. Note the following examples:

- A wife accuses her husband of showing no interest in her. She says he ignores her feelings and relational needs. He responds by saying, "I don't know where you come up with these complaints."

- A woman suffers from many physical ailments such as headaches and nervous stomach. In spite of the evidence that no biological impetus is causing these ailments, she refuses to believe they are due to pent-up emotions.

- Even though an adult has persistent problems loving fellow adults, she claims to have an ideal family history.

- When a negative trait such as irritability is exposed, the person immediately excuses it by saying, "I'm normally not this way. I really have an optimistic spirit."

- Rather than seeing their own contributions to family conflicts, parents can persistently focus on the child's misbehavior, asking, "Why are you so stubborn?"

The inherent fear in denial is that our humanness or vulnerability might be discovered and held against us. When we deny our problems, we insinuate, *It could be disastrous to admit imperfections; I'd hate to think what that would do to my reputation.*

■ ■ ■ ■

How are you inclined to use denial? *(For instance, in marital arguments I rarely admit my problems because I'm too busy focusing on my partner's problems.)*

1. _____

   _____

   _____

2. _____

   _____

   _____

3. _____

   _____

   _____

■ ■ ■ ■

Evasiveness is different from denial in that evasiveness is driven by a conscious element of fear, while denial involves subconscious self-deception. Evasiveness is a *deliberate* deception of others. When we act evasively, we are specifically choosing to avoid the responsibility of meeting problems head on. We assume that open conflicts or confrontations would be uncomfortable. Examples abound:

- A wife knows her upset husband wants to discuss a delicate family matter with her. She dislikes conflict so much she decides to stay away from the house to avoid the discussion—and the problem.

- A worker disagrees with his superior's policy decision. But instead of openly talking about it with the supervisor, he complains to others.

- A teenager doesn't want to hear his parents' suggestions, so when they try to talk with him he clams up.

- A woman talks to her girlfriend about her struggles with depression. The friend doesn't like talking about a negative subject so she looks for the first opportunity to change the subject.

When we are evasive, we may be fearfully wondering, *What if I say the wrong thing? You might not like me if I tell you what I really feel. I am inadequately equipped to discuss personal matters.* Evasiveness is a mark of personal insecurity and a lack of trust in others.

■ ■ ■ ■

What forms of evasiveness have you used recently? *(For instance, I'd like to talk to my parents about their control over me, but it might be difficult, so I keep our conversations very superficial.)*

1. _____

   _____

2. _____

   _____

3. _____

   _____

■ ■ ■ ■

Reversal, the third general style of defensiveness, is more openly combative. It is driven by the idea that the best way to protect yourself is to keep others on the defensive. When we use reversal techniques, we assume others are out to get us, so we become offensive whenever delicate matters are mentioned. Here are some examples:

- When a wife tells her husband he spoke rudely to a family member, he shouts back, "Let's talk about the time you openly criticized me in front of everyone. Now *that* was rude!"

- When a ten-year-old girl tells her mom she is hurt because of her mother's harsh words, the mother replies, "Well maybe next time you'll show more respect and this won't happen."

A woman accuses her sister of being insensitive. When the sister asks for patience because she has been under unusual stress, the woman retorts, "Every time I try to talk to you about our differences you come up with a lame excuse, and you try to make me out to be the bad guy."

A husband complains that his wife seems disinterested in him. She answers, "If only you were more easygoing, I might be able to accommodate you."

Growing relationships need openness and accountability; that means we sometimes need to address flaws. But when these flaws arise, our fears can prompt us to keep others from being too confrontational by threatening to put *them* in the hot seat. The result is a major breakdown in communication.

■ ■ ■ ■

How do you use reversal to defend yourself? *(For instance, when a family member tells me about a mistake I made, I give a quick rebuttal.)*

1. _____

_____

_____

2. _____

_____

_____

3. _____

_____

_____

■ ■ ■ ■

As Diane talked about her defenses with Dr. Minirth, she admitted, "I use all those defensive techniques and more, particularly in my closest relationships."

"Can you see how it creates the anger you so desperately wish to avoid?" he asked.

"Well, I know it only creates greater frustration, if that's what you mean. Then comes that self-perpetuating cycle I mentioned. The other person becomes more disenchanted, then I become even more defensive, and so on."

> Being authentic does not require us to deny our fears. It means we will erect minimal barriers and have little to hide.

Dr. Minirth explained, "If you want to reduce your episodes of anger, you'll need to let go of your fears. You're letting other people have too much power over you. You can introduce healthier qualities to your relationships."

BECOMING AUTHENTIC

The opposite of fearful defense is open authenticity. This means while we are wise enough to balance self-disclosures, we are also willing to make ourselves as known as common sense allows. Authenticity is living without pretense; our external lives are consistent with our internal lives. Being authentic does not require us to deny our fears; there is enough imperfection to warrant some wariness in each of us. It means we will erect minimal barriers and have little to hide.

Check the following statements you can agree with.

- ☐ It's not necessary for others to accept all my opinions; I can let them disagree.

- ☐ When someone sees my weakness, our relationship can become closer.

- ☐ Even when I disagree with a family member's perspective about me, we can still share a sense of companionship.

- ☐ Sharing personal preferences and emotions is a goal I would like to attain.

☐ I don't want to be known as a combatant, but I believe it can be important to share my disagreements openly.

☐ I want to have a good reputation but not at the expense of honesty and accountability.

The more statements you were able to check, the more likely you are able to live without excessive fear.

To be authentic we must accept ourselves, who we are. This is what caused Diane to consider how her fears were depriving her of emotional composure. She told Dr. Minirth, "I'm so careful to check others' reactions to me that I constantly doubt myself."

"By letting fear guide you," said Dr. Minirth, "you are inviting people to think poorly of you."

"But how is that? I mean, I'm not wearing a sign that says 'kick me,'" she said with a smile.

"You may as well be wearing one. When people sense your hesitancy or your defensiveness, they are prone to reject you. You'll get the adverse treatment you don't want. Then you become angry, which only makes matters worse."

Diane thought for a moment, then said, "Letting go of my fears would represent a real change for me. You're suggesting I quit caring so much about everybody's feelings about me and just cut loose."

"With discretion, of course," he replied. "I'm operating on the assumption that you can afford to be real. I don't see you as someone who is so awful you have to assume everyone will dislike you."

■ ■ ■ ■

Think about the relationships that bring out your fearful defenses. How would authenticity cause you to be different? *(For instance, I wouldn't expend as much energy rationalizing to my friends why I make the choices I do.)*

1. _____

_____

_____

2. _____

_____

_____

Now consider how authenticity will diminish your inclination toward anger. You would be less annoyed at others' feelings or reactions because you would not be so consumed with keeping your safe cover. As a result, what would change in your lifestyle? *(For instance, I'd have more patience because I'd quit obsessing about how my family ought to feel about me.)*

1. _____

_____

_____

2. _____

_____

_____

■ ■ ■ ■

Realizing she could hardly afford to continue in her current self-doubt, Diane decided it was time to overhaul her style of relating. She was learning that as long as she assumed others could not be trusted, that assumption became a self-fulfilling prophecy; the result would be ongoing anger. These were some of her adjustments:

■ She would be more transparent in her communication with other women. Rather than trying to appear as though she had no cares in the world, she would not have to hide her insecurities or needs.

■ Even as she exposed her humanness, she could also convey a confidence in herself by eliminating her tendency to apologize for how she felt. Her demeanor would simply communicate, *I am what I am.*

■ When a man was friendly toward her, she would not immediately assume he was conniving. She resolved to be forceful enough to turn down an inappropriate advance if it really became necessary.

- When she was criticized by her parents, particularly her father, she did not have to defend herself. She acknowledged he would probably always be hardheaded, but that didn't mean her value was any less.

- If she was with people who seemed more socially adept than she was, that would be okay. She did not have to pressure herself to be someone she was not.

By deciding to let go of fearful behaviors, Diane found she had less emotional garbage inside. As a result, when time came for legitimate anger, it was not tainted by excessive insecurities.

WHY WE STRUGGLE WITH FEAR

Our fearful tendencies are usually learned from childhood or current experiences with significant people in our lives. To set fears aside it is good to understand what creates them.

We Overinterpret Rejection

From the beginning, God ordained human relationships to be a haven. Whether it is parent and child, friend to friend, spouse to spouse, or sibling to sibling, each relationship functions to convey honor and respect to those involved. God always has a purpose in what He designs. In relationships, the purpose is to underscore human dignity.

But having said that, we must also admit that many relationships do not even remotely resemble God's purpose. Sinful pride can make a relationship far more detrimental than uplifting. This can cause us to panic, thinking, *Oh no! My relationships have turned sour. I'm being rejected. I can't handle it!* Then we allow rejection to debilitate us until we assume that peace and stability are completely out of reach. Examples of this are shown in the following illustrations:

- A wife fears if she tells her husband what she really thinks, he will leave her. So she fearfully represses her needs, assuming his rejection would render her helpless and hopeless.

- A mother is afraid if she is too strong in disciplining her son, he will not like her. She compromises her principles so they can have peace.

- An employee thinks if he shows uniqueness, his supervisor will reprimand him, leaving him with job insecurity.

In each of these illustrations, the potential for rejection leads to the interpretation, *If I let someone down, it would be the end of me.*

■ ■ ■ ■

When have you felt this way? *(For instance, I'd like to tell my mother she interferes with our lifestyle, but she'd make my life miserable if I said that, so I don't say anything.)*

1. _____

_____

_____

2. _____

_____

_____

■ ■ ■ ■

When we overinterpret rejections, we are not only guilty of letting others have too much power, we also are communicating *I can't trust myself.* That lack of self-trust is noticed by others, giving them "permission" to pounce. It's a self-fulfilling prophecy.

Wanting Diane to back away from her fears, Dr. Minirth said, "Looking at your past, we can find many reasons for your fears. Your parents did not create an environment conducive to real sharing, and you learned there were many judges in your world who would reject you if you did something wrong. It became safer just to keep your feelings to yourself."

"But in the long run that hasn't helped," she replied. "I've been bottling up anger, and it's eating me alive."

"Diane, we've discussed how you can afford to be more assertive with your needs. But before this can work, you need to ask yourself, *Are my emotions trustworthy?*"

"Well I can already tell you I'm not a blatantly selfish or insensitive person," she replied. "When I have things to share, they usually have legitimacy."

Dr. Minirth encouraged her by saying, "If that is the case, you need to worry less about people rejecting or invalidating your feelings as you speak them. Hold firmly to your inner convictions rather than deferring to someone else's agendas.

"True assertiveness is anchored in the confidence that you are a legitimate person with legitimate needs," he continued. "You don't have to let another's rejection be the final word," he told her.

Once you learn to place more trustworthiness in your own assertiveness and bow less to others' rejections, you'll notice changes in the way you express your needs.

- You can state your preferences without having to give several justifications for them.

- When someone attempts to invalidate your feelings, you need not enter a power play. You can let others be invalidating even as you confidently stand your ground.

- While you attempt to be sensitive as you speak assertively, you do not worry so much about ruffling others' feathers that you never communicate real feelings.

■ ■ ■ ■

How would your anger management be different if you worried less about rejection and placed more trust in your assertions? *(For instance, I would speak more pointedly about my feelings rather than vaguely beating around the bush.)*

1. _____

_____

_____

2. _____

_____

_____

■ ■ ■ ■ ■

No one likes to be rejected. But we can decide that responsible openness has priority over repression of emotions. Knowing we are honestly trying to be constructive, we can afford to be authentic.

We Are Uncertain of Others' Motives

An ideal relationship creates security. It is built upon trustworthiness, acceptance, and servitude. When this ideal is met, fear is negligible. Openness and vulnerability not only are low-risk factors in this relationship, they are natural.

But people like Diane, who have had less-than-ideal relationships, live with fears because they assume the relationship will include factors other than trustworthiness, acceptance, or servitude. Experience has taught them other people are capable of deception or condescension or selfishness. Defensiveness becomes the norm that makes them vulnerable to anger.

Diane once explained it this way: "Why should I let down my guard? In the past I've learned that people don't really care about my needs. They have their own hidden agendas, and if I become vulnerable I'll just play into their hands."

"Can you give me an example of this?" asked Dr. Minirth.

"A couple of years ago I was best friends with a woman, and I felt I could tell her anything . . . which is precisely what I did. But I later learned she gossiped about me to her other friends, making me look foolish."

"What a letdown," said Dr. Minirth. "What you thought was a successful relationship turned out to be a major disappointment. Apparently this woman used your self-disclosures to make herself seem superior in the eyes of others."

"That's the point. But how could I have known she would do that? She seemed sincere when we first became acquainted."

■ ■ ■ ■

Fear exists because of the unknowns in other persons' personalities. Can we really trust them? When they say they love us, can we be sure? What experiences have you had that left you feeling disillusioned like this? *(For instance, I once told a friend about a major mistake I had made, and he later used it against me when we had a disagreement.)*

1. _____

_____

_____

2. _____

_____

_____

■ ■ ■ ■

You can see how this fearfulness can keep anger alive. When we eye others suspiciously, we maintain an edge of harshness. Our self-preservation mode kicks into high gear, and we interpret others' motives with cynicism. This creates a pessimistic, even imprisoning, manner of relating.

Dr. Minirth disclosed to Diane, "I'm just stubborn enough not to let my emotions be dictated by others. I assume that no one will ever be completely trustworthy, yet I can choose independently to maintain inner balance in spite of it. Can you adopt such a mind-set?"

"That would be unnatural," she replied. "I guess I'm so busy reading the motives behind someone else's behavior I neglect my own independent game plan."

"It may sound pessimistic for me to suggest this," said Dr. Minirth, "but if you accept the idea that a person can have less than the highest motives in relating with you, you'll not be shocked when a disappointment occurs. The result will be that you won't give undue attention to someone else's failings and you can stay on your course for healthy living."

■ ■ ■ ■

What about you? What shocks you in your closest relationships? *(For instance, I was shocked when my son said he hated me.)*

1. _____

   _____

   _____

2. _____

   _____

   _____

If you let go of your shock (and its associated fear), you will be guided by objectivity. This will allow you to respond without preexisting assumptions about the treatment you should receive. How might objectivity positively affect your emotional disposition? *(For instance, when my son tells me he hates me, I can tell him that we have a lot to discuss then. I'll hear him without invalidating his feelings.)*

1. _____

   _____

2. _____

   _____

■ ■ ■ ■

When we stop trying to control others' "behind-the-scenes" feelings, we react less and are thus freed to initiate our own healthy response pattern.

We Forget God Is in Charge

The psalmist wrote: "In God I have put my trust; I will not fear. What can flesh do to me?" (Psalm 56:4). When our emotions hinge on the opinions of humans, we are fearful because

> In God I have put my trust; I will not fear. What can flesh do to me?
> —Psalm 56:4

we can never be sure when we might be rejected or criticized or ignored. A human-based self-image is only as secure as the humans we entrust with our emotions. But a God-based self-image is different. Because God accepts us, weaknesses and all, we can live confidently in the knowledge that He can guide us through all relational or circumstantial pitfalls.

Notice how a person can gain self-esteem when he or she lets God be in charge of emotional stability.

- A father fears his teenage son is being influenced by the wrong crowd. This tempts him to be very angry. Yet he is reminded that God's means of discipline is laced with love and gentle firmness. So the father chooses to speak to his son in this godly fashion, knowing it will be better.

- A wife senses her husband is losing interest in her. Perhaps there is another woman. Rather than panicking, she remains confident in the knowledge that God will allow no burden to befall her that she cannot bear.

- A woman is timid in social situations. But rather than letting people have a godlike ability to dictate her self-esteem, she remembers that God does not require her to be a social gadfly before He can accept her.

- A man has an intimidating boss who is free with his criticism. The man decides he can only do his best, and if the boss still criticizes, he will not be so devastated that he loses the ability to concentrate on his duties.

Drawing upon God's strength requires a God focus rather than a human focus. We can choose to let our emotions be dictated by humans' opinions or God's opinion.

Diane told Dr. Minirth, "I know it is best to trust in God, but this will not come naturally for me."

"If you had received godly love from your primary role models, your parents, you wouldn't be struggling so much to grasp God's empowerment," said Dr. Minirth. "I know it will feel awkward initially to redirect your thinking, but it can be done."

They discussed some ways she could be more trusting in God.

- When she read Scripture, she would personalize its redemptive message, as though God had written it just for her.

- Her prayers would not just be the "help me" variety. She would openly recount to God His characteristics that gave her hope. Prayer would be a time for worshiping Him.

- She would take risks with fellow Christians and let herself be known and loved by them.

- She would specify the godly traits she needed to incorporate into her life. Then she would pick situations where she could choose to use those traits.

■ ■ ■ ■

How about you? What would change in your life if you become less consumed with fears and more consumed with God's guidance? *(For instance, when I discipline my kids I would be less worried that they might disobey. I'd speak with calm assurance.)*

1. _____

_____

_____

2. _____

_____

_____

9

∷ Loneliness Creates Anger

■ **Step 9. Accept the inevitability of loneliness as you struggle to be understood.**

From the beginning of time God intended for us to maintain close ties with family and friends. "It is not good that man should be alone," He declared (Genesis 2: 18). So God gave Adam the gift of a relationship to prevent loneliness. Although Adam and his wife created problems for themselves by disobeying God, His original tenet continues to hold true. We

> **It is not good that man should be alone.**
> —Genesis 2:18

were not created to be forever alone. Experienced to the extreme, being alone agitates our emotions.

Consider some of the many pleasant ways we connect with others:

- At a store we like the clerk to be friendly and considerate of our preferences.

- We enjoy chatting with our children, knowing they appreciate the feelings we are trying to convey.

- We want our churches to have an atmosphere that says, *Humanness is accepted here.*

- Though we are expected to maintain a standard of excellence in our work, we appreciate a smile and an occasional pat on the back.

- We are comforted when we sense that our spouse understands our mood, even though words are not exchanged.

- We feel warm inside after a friend calls just to inquire how we are doing.

We like to feel connected. Without this feeling our emotions shout in protest, *Hey, I don't like being all alone. Won't someone pay attention to me?* Loneliness makes us vulnerable to anger. As you consider the causes for your anger, you can ask yourself, *Do I have any habits or tendencies that keep me in an unwanted pit of isolation?*

Laura was a thirty-two-year-old mother of three. Slender and perky, she easily presented an image of friendliness. "I like being helpful to others," she told Dr. Carter. "I'm not the type who sits still, waiting for things to happen. I like to create activity. Connecting with my friends has always been important to me."

"But when you called for an appointment, you told my secretary you've had some major relationship problems," said Dr. Carter. "I assume you feel lacking in your ability to connect."

"That's my problem. All my life I've been a people-oriented person. But somehow it's never produced the satisfaction I've hoped for. My parents live near me, and neither of them shares the same relationship goals I do. Dad has always been a success in his work, and his greatest delight comes from being financially secure. He has friends, but he'd be just as happy if he didn't hear from them for a long time. Mother is shy and nervous. She has never felt comfortable in a crowd. So she can't relate to my social needs at all."

"You're insinuating, then, that in your years of relating with your original family, you have not felt as close as you might like because they're on such different wavelengths."

"That's right," said Laura. "I wish so much that I could just sit and talk with them about my feelings. But they truly don't know how to relate to me. We love each other, but there's a void that's very uncomfortable."

"Are they the only ones you feel this way about?"

"No. My husband, Brian, is from the same mold as my father. He's driven to succeed in his work, but he has no clue about how to relate to a woman. I try to talk with him about simple things . . . the kids' activities, my involvement in community groups. But honestly, I might as well be talking to a stump! He's out of it when it comes to relating."

"I imagine that creates real irritation in you," Dr. Carter responded. "As communicative as you are, it's probably the height of frustration when someone gives you little in return."

Sighing deeply, Laura nodded. "Sometimes I cry when I can't get through to Brian or my parents. Sometimes I get so mad I want to rage at them. It's tearing me up inside. And what's worse, I have an older sister who constantly feeds me advice about accepting people for what they are. I know she's right, but what am I going to do with my emotions? I'm too stirred up inside to just blindly accept!"

On the surface, Laura's family would conclude she had problems with anger. They would point to her temperamental nature or her easy frustration and say she needed to learn to be less grouchy. But her problem was not that simple. Before she could tame her anger, she needed to identify and manage her loneliness.

When Dr. Carter suggested Laura needed to explore her struggles with loneliness, a puzzled look crossed her face. "But I told you I know lots of people. Being social has never been a problem for me."

"Loneliness is more than just a measure of your social skills," he explained. "It is the emotion of isolation. It is the empty feeling that comes when we sense a companion is having difficulty relating to our feelings or perceptions. Loneliness is the uncomfortable awareness that gaps exist in our relationships."

To be lonely, you don't have to sit in a dark room staring into empty space. Solitude and loneliness are entirely different subjects. Perhaps you can recall a frustrating time when your family could not understand an idea you were explaining. Or maybe there has been an uncomfortable moment when you did not know how to respond to a hurting friend. When a lack of cohesion occurs in a relationship or when serious misunderstandings hamper communication, loneliness begins. It is the feeling that says, *We're in very different worlds.*

To determine if you have struggled with loneliness, check the following statements that apply to you.

- ☐ At times I feel I do not really fit in with the group I am in.

- ☐ I sometimes complain that the people in my most important relationships don't really understand me.

- ☐ I find myself yearning to be with someone other than the person I am with.

- ☐ Acceptance from others does not come as frequently as I would like.

- ☐ Something seems to be missing in my relationships.

- ☐ Many of my conversations lack subjective elements, such as discussion of emotions.

- ☐ I become frustrated because I seem to work harder at keeping relationships going than my friends or relatives do.

- ☐ People who know me in public don't really see how I struggle privately with my hurts.

- ☐ The persons I want to be closest to do not share my relational goals.

- ☐ Sometimes I withdraw from people because then I don't feel as much pain.

If you checked five or more statements, you probably have significant problems with loneliness and find yourself susceptible to frequent disgust, resentment, or disillusionment.

When Dr. Carter explained to Laura how loneliness is widely shown, she nodded. "I've felt estranged from significant people, but I didn't realize I had a problem with loneliness. I just told myself I was discouraged. But now I see it's really more accurate to say I have felt lonely . . . many times."

"By identifying loneliness accurately, Laura, you can take a major step toward corralling your anger. In our discussions we'll talk about ways to present your anger more responsibly. But to adjust your communication more realistically, we'll need to decide what to do with the loneliness that feeds your anger in the first place."

They identified loneliness at the base of several recent expressions of her anger:

- She had scolded Brian for being so disinterested when she had tried to initiate a friendly conversation. Deeper than her anger, though, was the realization that they had drifted so far apart.

- She became angry when her father gave her unwanted advice about her parenting methods. On a deeper level she was thinking how much she wished they could talk about affirming subjects.

- When socializing with girlfriends, she felt awkward as she sensed they had better marriages than she did. In loneliness, she wished they could understand how she hungered for a better life.

Because her sister's life seemed tension-free, Laura rarely discussed personal struggles with her. She realized she had been frustrated in the past by her sister's unawareness, but now Laura could admit she was also struggling from the loneliness of feeling emotionally alienated from her sister.

■ ■ ■ ■

How about you? What incidents of anger in your life indicate a deeper struggle with loneliness? *(For instance, I become annoyed at coworkers because they misunderstand my family life, but really I am lonely because they don't know me as well as they think they do.)*

1. _____

_____

_____

2. _____

_____

_____

▪ WHY WE FEEL LONELY

Angry people feel lonely because they sense gaps in their relationships. They could help curb their anger by understanding what causes the gaps. Some of the possible causes are spiritual disease, neglecting relationships, and failure to state our needs successfully. Let's look at each of these possibilities in detail.

Our Sinful Nature

Loneliness is as ancient as humanity's sinful nature. In modern psychology it is fashionable to say we feel lonely because of frustrated relationships or painful pasts or poor social skills. These explanations offer a partial understanding of loneliness, but they are not sufficient. Ultimately, we feel lonely because sin causes us to be estranged from God and thus inhibited from fully knowing and experiencing contentment.

In Chapters 4 and 7 we explored how control and pride began with Adam's fall into sin. One of the first emotional repercussions of that fall was loneliness. In fear, Adam hid from God and from his wife. He was ashamed to reveal himself fully. Looking for ways to cover up his vulnerabilities, he became evasive and phony.

> Ultimately, we feel lonely because sin causes us to be estranged from God and thus inhibited from fully knowing and experiencing contentment.

It can be fun to picture what life must have been like for Adam and Eve prior to sin. Created in God's image and unstained by imperfection at that point, we can assume they knew no lonely feelings. Instead, they were filled with godly qualities like love, joy, peace, and patience. Feeling connected was no problem. Adam must have been a master communicator who knew just the right things to say to make his wife feel special. Eve must have had a pleasantness that caused Adam to feel enthusiastic about being with her.

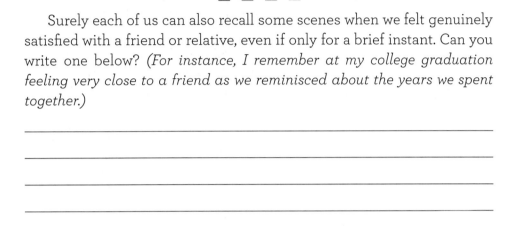

Surely each of us can also recall some scenes when we felt genuinely satisfied with a friend or relative, even if only for a brief instant. Can you write one below? *(For instance, I remember at my college graduation feeling very close to a friend as we reminisced about the years we spent together.)*

_____

_____

_____

_____

Our positive experiences give us a brief glimpse of what Adam and Eve must have experienced in abundance in their garden home.

But sin changed all that. After defying God, Adam realized he could not count on his mate to be fully reliable. *She tricked me,* he must have believed. And Eve must have thought, *If I am fully open to my spouse, he may use it against me. We're not as close as we used to be.* The very estrangement God wanted to avoid had come into their lives permanently. It even affected their connectedness with God as they realized how their fellowship with Him was now strained, at best.

Since then, every person has experienced the same emotional fallout as this original couple felt in the garden. We cannot get around it. Feelings of isolation are inevitable in each of us.

But by linking loneliness to our sinful nature, we are saying this emotion is natural to every person, with no exceptions. Some people experience it more intensely than others, but no one can hope for full exemption. From the earliest days of childhood to the last years of life, we will experience some form of loneliness.

Laura listened as Dr. Carter explained the inevitability of loneliness. Then she said, "It seems rather negative to say no one is immune from this emotion."

"I can't argue with you on that point," he replied. "It *is* a negative thought. But if you can accept its inevitability, you won't feel so surprised when you have lonely experiences. It's when you think you can completely avoid loneliness that it becomes unbearable."

"I've never thought of it like that," she mused. "Are you suggesting I can gain a victory over loneliness by first accepting my vulnerability to it?"

"That's correct," said Dr. Carter. "Let me give you an analogy. I have gimpy knees due to surgeries several years ago. They hurt sometimes, but like it or not I can't make that pain go away. Now, I have a choice in how to respond to the pain. Will I moan and groan about it, or will I accept it and go on with my day?"

"I see where you're going. You can complain about your loss and increase your awareness of the pain. Or you can continue with your day knowing the pain won't completely control you."

"Let's apply that mind-set to your response to loneliness," Dr. Carter continued. "There will be times when you feel isolated from others. If you choose not to accept your circumstances, anger will follow and your emotional pain will increase. Or you can choose to accept the unfortunate imperfection while also resolving to maintain contact with others as best as you can."

Most of us want to avoid emotional (as well as physical) pain. We dread being rejected or ignored or invalidated. Yet it is an unavoidable truth that this kind of pain can and will occur. Accepting this truth will not eliminate the pain, but it will render it less powerful.

Realizing that loneliness is an inevitable by-product of living in an imperfect world, Laura made some major adjustments in her key relationships.

- She decided it was wise to continue speaking with her husband about her needs and preferences, but she did not delude herself by expecting him to suddenly change his personality to suit her.

- When it was clear that her older sister was so full of criticism they could not connect relationally, she ceased her attempts to force the sister into a more compassionate, understanding mode.

- When her parents seemed displeased with a decision she made about her children, she reminded herself she did not have to have their approval before proceeding with good parenting skills.

- If a friend gave her simplistic and unsolicited advice about her marriage, she was consoled by remembering that perfect cohesion was not necessary to maintain that friendship.

By accepting the reality of her loneliness, Laura's feelings of isolation did not disappear. But she was less angry. She no longer fumed that people were unfair. Instead, she concluded she would do what she could to promote relational harmony while realizing the pain might reappear.

■ ■ ■ ■

If you became less threatened by relational pain, how would your anger be affected? *(For instance, I would worry less when my children disagreed with me, and I would focus instead on being fair but firm.)*

1. _____

_____

_____

2. _____

_____

_____

■ ■ ■ ■

We Neglect Relationships

While loneliness can partially be explained by our sinful nature, it can also be blamed, in part, on neglected relationships. We can be so busy with work and activities that we put too little emphasis on the more important stuff of living, such as empathy or authenticity or bearing burdens.

Laura readily acknowledged this fact with Dr. Carter one day. "I'm always so preoccupied with trying to keep my children going I hardly have time for my own needs. Each day is filled with errands and taxiing kids to their various activities. I can hardly imagine how career women with children manage their lives!"

Dr. Carter replied, "Reading between the lines, I'm hearing you say you would like to share some personally rewarding time with other adults, but it's hard to carve out the time."

"You got that right! And even when I'm with friends, we just compare notes about our busy schedules instead of really engaging in any deeper level of sharing."

Seeking additional insights, Dr. Carter asked, "Can you see the implications this has for loneliness? I imagine you regularly experience anger and frustration. But the anger is caused, in part, by your ongoing lack of meaningful dialogue with others. You have too much empty activity."

Being too busy is not the only way to neglect relational growth. We can also be lazy about expending the energy necessary to maintain satisfactory ties with others.

To determine whether you sometimes create your own loneliness by neglecting your relationships, check the following items that apply to you.

- ☐ I am sometimes reluctant to let friends or family members know about my personal struggles.

- ☐ When someone talks to me, I can easily be distracted by activities occurring near us.

- ☐ When someone expresses his or her feelings, I'd rather talk about the solutions than hear more about what causes those feelings.

- ☐ I know I should carve out more time for close friendships, but I seem to procrastinate.

- ☐ Even when I'm with people in a relaxed setting, I'm too concerned about making proper impressions.

- ☐ I have many pressing activities that constantly keep me from feeling at ease.

- ☐ It has been too long since I last sat down with friends to share personal problems.

- ☐ At times I try to avoid people because I don't want to be hassled.

If you checked four or more items, you are probably digging your own hole of loneliness. You may need to spend more time in nurturing satisfactory relationships.

■ ■ ■ ■

What tendencies keep you from enjoying depth in your relationships? *(For instance, I tend to talk to my friends about trivial or superficial matters; I know I should be less concerned about activities and more concerned about relationships, but I don't make that adjustment.)*

1. _____

_____

_____

2. _____

_____

_____

3. _____

_____

_____

■ ■ ■ ■

During Jesus' ministry, He was approached by a young lawyer who asked Jesus to tell him the ultimate aim of life. Christ's response was that we are to love God with all our heart, soul, and mind, and we are to love our neighbors as ourselves. In this succinct answer He testified that our foremost goal is to relate first with God, then with others.

As simple as Christ's philosophy may seem, most of us are easily sidetracked in applying it, if we think of it at all. Other matters take precedence . . . impressing people, achieving career goals, meeting schedules.

■ ■ ■ ■

What priorities do you have that hinder deeper relationships? *(For instance, my perfectionism causes me to consider cleanliness more important than kindness; I worry too much about saying the right things.)*

1. _____
   _____
   _____

2. _____
   _____
   _____

■ ■ ■ ■

As Laura considered her self-inflicted loneliness, she said, "Things will have to change drastically if I am going to get out of my rut."

"What do you mean?"

"Well, I've told myself a hundred times that I should slow down long enough to stay in touch with the people I love. But my good intentions always seem to get pushed aside. Some activity always gets in the way."

"Your priorities will have to be rearranged to make these adjustments," said Dr. Carter. "I think we would both agree you'll always have personal responsibilities that will keep you busy. But you can manage your obligations while also making time to nurture your relationships. The net result should be less anger and tension; being in touch with others should boost your moods significantly."

To lessen her feelings of isolation, Laura made several lifestyle adjustments:

- On the telephone or in person, she talked less about trivial matters. She was determined to let people see more clearly who she really was.

- She became less consumed with forcing her children to fit her mold and more concerned about encouraging them to talk about their feelings.

- Realizing her husband would never be a great communicator, she decided not to get caught in the depressing habit of criticism. Instead, she would encourage him whenever she could and have minimal expectations of how he ought to respond.

She carved out time each week to have fun with a friend, knowing it was important to have ongoing experiences that kept her close to others.

◼ ◼ ◼ ◻

As you consider the adjustments you could make to reduce your loneliness, what specifics come to mind? *(For instance, I could get my kids to bed early enough that my spouse and I could have time together; I could call that friend who has been wanting to go to lunch with me.)*

1. _____

   _____

   _____

2. _____

   _____

   _____

◼ ◼ ◼ ◻

Giving relationships higher priority will not make your anger disappear entirely, but it will keep you from obsessing about why you feel so unappreciated or unnoticed by others.

We Do Not State Our Needs Successfully

Loneliness-based anger arises when we sense that others care little about our personal needs. Usually we fume, *Why can't people just understand who I am?* Yet careful examination often shows we expect others to guess correctly what we want. This can only lead to ongoing frustration because most of our friends and relatives—like most people everywhere—do not read minds well. This problem was at the heart of Laura's anger.

Dr. Carter told her, "You've said you feel alienated from family members because they don't know you as well as they should. Perhaps you could be more direct in telling these people how they can respond to those needs."

"I've tried, but I get no good results. My husband doesn't listen to me, and my parents are too busy trying to fix me to hear what I say. Talking does no good."

"I agree there's no guarantee you can force others to respond properly to your needs," said Dr. Carter. "But I still suspect you could find more successful ways of communicating them to others."

"How could I do that?"

"First, let me ask if you get caught in a couple of detrimental communication patterns. One is using too much salesmanship as you speak, and the other is trying to justify your needs too strongly when they are questioned. Does either of those situations ever happen?"

"Just about every time. I never feel like I'm taken seriously when I speak."

"I want you to notice something related to this," said Dr. Carter. "When you try too hard to persuade others that your needs are legitimate, or if you defend your position too powerfully, they get the idea that you lack confidence in what you are saying. The net result is they don't seriously consider your needs, and this leaves you feeling disconnected and then angry."

"But what could I do differently?"

"You could start by taking the insistence out of your voice. When you have a legitimate need, state it in an even tone of voice and be succinct. Then if your need is invalidated or questioned, don't defend it. Just say, 'Nonetheless, that's how I feel.' If you engage in a power play, you create the adversarial climate that leads to strong feelings of estrangement."

"But what if I'm still not taken seriously?" asked Laura.

"Then you're no worse off than you would have been if you had pleaded your case unnecessarily. There is no guarantee others will respond to your needs once you've shared them. But by presenting yourself in a more composed manner at least you will not receive the rejection as powerfully."

■ ■ ■ ■

By communicating in an abrasive or insecure manner we create the very loneliness that makes our anger worse. Can you think of times when you create a gulf in a major relationship that leaves you feeling angry? *(For instance, when I talk with my son about house rules, I can quickly alienate him by being too condescending.)*

1. _____

_____

_____

2. _____

_____

_____

■ ■ ■ ■

Most of us know when we are communicating in a way that creates the very relationship rifts we do not want. Yet we dig ourselves into these holes anyway. This is usually caused by weariness from having to take the lead to make relationships work when we wish others would take the initiative. We complain, "It's just not fair. I'm always the one reaching out to others."

> Successful anger management requires a willingness to come out of our shells and be known.

If we assume that relationships should always respect rules of fairness, we delude ourselves. People can be grossly unfair. And by wishing otherwise we fail to accept reality; the result is muddled emotions. Rather than wishing aimlessly for fairness, we can minimize our anger by taking the initiative to bridge the gulfs that disrupt relationships. This is what Laura determined to do in her life:

- She would be more immediate in addressing the needs that others seemed to ignore.

- Accepting inevitable estrangement in some of her closest relationships, she resolved to initiate discussions of feelings and relational goals.

- Rather than inwardly complaining to herself that others didn't really know her, she made it a point to keep people informed about the intricacies of her lifestyle.

■ ■ ■ ■

How about you? What adjustments could you make to more successfully address your relational needs? *(For instance, rather than just wishing my coworkers would understand how they could better blend with my schedule, I can coach them about my work habits.)*

1. _____

_____

_____

2. _____

_____

_____

■ ■ ■ ■

In this chapter we have seen that, rather than remaining in a rut of isolation and loneliness, we can choose to minimize this problem by adjusting our thoughts and activities. Successful anger management requires a willingness to come out of our shells and be known.

10

▪▪ Anger Reflects
Inferiority Feelings

▪ Step 10. Relate to others as equals,
neither elevating yourself above them nor
accepting a position of inferiority.

Russ had been in counseling long enough to identify his anger correctly and to direct his efforts toward more productive ways of communicating it. He was married and had a teenage son by a previous marriage and two teenage stepdaughters. "Having three teenagers under one roof is enough to keep my anger going for a while," he would joke.

His initial reason for seeing Dr. Carter was to seek help in learning to resolve family disputes in a more even manner. Russ admitted he became too volatile once he lost control of his emotions. "Most of the time I'm pretty successful at just letting things roll off my back. But once in a while something sets me off and I turn into a madman for a few moments. I can be pretty intimidating."

When asked for a few examples of this behavior, he shared some common scenarios:

- When his son was slow in getting chores done, Russ sometimes shouted, "Why do I have to follow you around with a prod to get some movement out of you?"

- When his wife had sheepishly confessed that she overspent her monthly budget, he angrily said, "Do you think I'm some kind of money machine? You've got to get with the program!"

- His stepdaughters' arguments over time in the bathroom prompted Russ to storm, "I didn't come home to hear this grumbling! I'm sick of all the tension around here."

"Sounds to me," said Dr. Carter, "that you have some legitimate frustrations, but you respond to them with quick sarcasm and condescension, and that only makes matters worse."

"I know I'm my own worst enemy sometimes. But I can't seem to contain myself. It's like something inside of me won't leave well enough alone. I don't know why I do what I do."

Dr. Carter thought for a moment, then said, "Russ, we had some earlier discussions about healthy versus unhealthy choices you can make to manage your anger. I know you are aware of the more appropriate path to take. So ignorance is not your problem. I'm thinking these anger episodes may reflect some fundamental problems in your self-esteem."

"Are you trying to tell me I'm insecure?"

"Let's put it this way . . . if you were genuinely secure, you'd be responding to these irritations with a clean style of assertiveness, not sarcasm. The way you manage your emotions is a commentary on your real self. When anger is out of bounds, it hints at a shaky ego."

Russ conceded, "I know I usually pretend I'm pretty self-secure, but I'd have to admit I sometimes get caught in personal doubts. So I'm open to your input."

"Think carefully," Dr. Carter continued. "Anger involves standing *up* for your basic needs, which implies that you feel you're in a *down* position at that moment."

"As if I'm discouraged because no one is showing respect to me?"

"Precisely. In its best use, anger elevates you from a low position to one of equality with the person who is being disrespectful. But when you feel too strongly compelled to stand up for your needs, I interpret that to mean you are struggling too powerfully with the feeling of being put down. Overused anger tells me you are struggling with the frustration of feeling lowly and inferior."

▪ EVERYONE FEELS INFERIOR AT TIMES

No one should be surprised to admit feeling inferior at times. We all have to contend with this problem. Because of our innate sinfulness, we all have some awareness that we do not measure up to God's perfect standards. Not all of us are so spiritually minded to link inferiority feelings to our position before God, but each person has wondered at some time, *Why do I fall short of the ideals of purest living?*

> Despite our good intentions, something keeps us from being the ultimate person. That something is our natural bent toward sin.

Think about your inadequacies for a moment. For example, have you ever questioned why you are often impatient in spite of your desire to be otherwise? Do you get caught in critical thinking patterns even though you want to be more positive? Have you treated family members insensitively and later regretted that you hadn't acted as kindly as you knew you should? We all have had many moments like these. Despite our good intentions, something keeps us from being the ultimate person. That something is our natural bent toward sin.

For example, Russ did not always feel inferior, but his angry, overblown reactions to what he perceived as his family's displays of disrespect hinted at a constant sense of insecurity within him.

■ ■ ■ ■

Respond to the following statements with your own examples:

I have recently fallen short of my ideal lifestyle by _____

_____

_____

I have good intentions to be helpful or considerate, but I get side-tracked by _____

_____

_____

I'd rather people not know that I _____

_____

_____

■ ■ ■ ■

Not only does our propensity for sin create feelings of uneasiness, it also gives us a natural tendency to compare ourselves to others. And sometimes, when we come up short, we are left holding on to inferiority. Think, for example, about a project that required a lot of time and effort. You gave it your best shot, but in the end someone noticed an error, or perhaps someone else completed a similar task more successfully. Your natural reaction probably prompted you to think, *Why didn't I do this job better?* or *What will it take to make others see how capable I really am?* It is almost impossible for us never to think of our comparative standing with others and wonder how we can achieve a competitive edge.

■ ■ ■ ■

What are some situations when you might feel you compare unfavorably to someone else? *(For instance, when my son speaks disrespectfully to me in front of my friends, I worry that I look foolish; my friend has less money than I do, yet I seem to manage mine less successfully.)*

1. _____

   _____

   _____

2. _____

   _____

   _____

■ ■ ■ ■

Sin gives us a natural tendency toward inferiority feelings; our environment, both past and present, can also inadvertently intensify its effect on us. In moderating your anger it can be helpful to be aware of two common traps: (1) the trap of succumbing to inferiority feelings and (2) the trap of attempting to be falsely superior. Either of these traps hampers our attempts at anger management.

We Succumb to Inferiority Feelings

Dr. Carter spoke with Russ about longstanding trends that kept his inferiority feelings alive. "I'm assuming when you were a boy you sometimes felt insecurity just as anyone else does. But can you remember any ongoing circumstances that enhanced those lowly feelings?"

"Well, a couple of examples come immediately to mind," he replied. "My dad made it clear that I had to be a cut above the crowd in my grades and in my behavior. He didn't really say a lot about my performance, but it was one of those things he didn't have to mention often. I knew I'd better excel to keep him happy."

"And if you didn't?"

"That created problems. I knew I wasn't as outstanding in some areas as he wanted me to be. So if I failed or even if I just came up a little short in a project, I'd feel guilty. I didn't want to let my dad know I was as human as I really was."

"In other words," said Dr. Carter, "you struggled with shame over being merely mortal."

"Right. So you can imagine how badly I felt when I really did do something wrong! I'd feel like I couldn't possibly let him see my error-prone ways."

"And I suppose this tendency carried over into your peer relationships?"

"It did, though not as strongly. I actually felt relieved to know my buddies didn't pitch a fit when I showed my weaknesses. But I can still recall moments when I cringed at the thought that they might see me fail."

Dr. Carter reflected, "Somehow you learned to think you were less than acceptable because of your humanness. That's what I mean when I say you may unnecessarily succumb to inferiority feelings."

Russ's memories are similar to those of many people we counsel. Maybe their self-esteem was tied closely to their latest performance. Or it could be they were treated unfairly by authorities. Or perhaps their unique ideas or feelings were just ignored. Whatever the situation, this unspoken message was always conveyed: *Remember, you're not as perfect as you should be.*

■ ■ ■ ■

What experiences kept you in the trap of inferiority feelings? *(For instance, my feelings of acceptance were only as strong as my latest performance; my sister seemed to handle problems so much easier than I did.)*

1. _____

_____

2. _____

_____

3. _____

_____

4. _____

_____

■ ■ ■ ■

The more you have been weighed down by reminders of your inadequacies, the more inclined you will be to harbor anger. As anger festers, an inner thought grows: *I'm really tired of being looked down upon. Something's got to give.* We differ in the ways we let this anger show. Some suppress it until depression or apathy sets in. Others develop a cynical edge that prompts adversarial remarks.

■ ■ ■ ■

Respond to the following statement.

When I feel like I don't measure up, I tend to _____

_____

_____

■ ■ ■ ■

We Seek False Superiority

Most of us are not content to wallow in lowly inadequacy; when feelings of inferiority come upon us, we look for a way out. The most common escape is to seek an edge of superiority. This practice is so common most of us are not consciously aware we are doing it. Yet we all have fallen into this trap many times. Consider the following examples:

- You respond to a family member's criticism by saying, "You don't even know what you're talking about!"

- A coworker is uncooperative, so behind his back you talk about his ineffectiveness on the job.

- You know you can't out-debate your spouse in a dispute, so you give him or her the silent treatment for several hours.

- When your child questions your decision, you speak very strongly in an attempt to intimidate him or her.

- You respond to a friend's personal problem by telling him or her how to handle it.

In each of these hypothetical illustrations you react to a frustration by attempting to gain an upper hand. Understandably, no one wants to be treated lowly, but instead of seeking equality when this happens we inwardly fume, *I'll show you who's better!*

To determine if you compensate for inferiority feelings with attempts to be superior, respond to the following items:

- ☐ I have a hard time listening to someone who is frustrated with me; I want to offer a rebuttal.
- ☐ When someone speaks ill of me, I respond in kind.
- ☐ I like to give the impression that I have fewer problems than I really do.
- ☐ When confronted by someone, I am likely to respond with a harsh put-down.
- ☐ I fret or worry too much when someone makes a decision that will directly affect me.
- ☐ I am known for being rigid or inflexible at times.
- ☐ I can quickly dissect a person's interpretations of me, putting that person on the defensive.
- ☐ Once I've developed an opinion, I don't want to waste time hearing alternate viewpoints.
- ☐ When someone does me wrong, I may stew for quite some time, wondering how to get even.

If you checked five or more of these statements you probably worry too much about your lowly standing in the eyes of others.

The roots to our attempts to be superior are in our childhood tendency toward competitiveness. Can you recall a typical conversation between two five-year-olds? One child says boastfully, "I get to go swimming today." And the other replies, "I've already been swimming two times this week." It's uncanny how children need to feel they have an edge over their peers, even when the issue is trivial.

Children intuitively realize they are not on the highest rung in their culture's pecking order. Many authorities can demand conformity from them. In one moment they will submit to another person's power. But an instant later they will attempt to buck the authority. Their behavior communicates, *Hey, it's my turn to have the upper hand around here. I'm tired of feeling like I've got no power.*

■ ■ ■ ▪

As you reflect on your childhood attempts to establish superiority, what common habits do you recall? *(For instance, when my older brother was mean to me, I became more forceful with my younger sister; when my parents told me what to do, I would point out the illogic in their requests.)*

1. _____

_____

_____

2. _____

_____

_____

■ ■ ■ ▪

This craving to be superior does not cease when we become adults. If anything, it intensifies because we have more options for manipulating others. Husbands and wives often respond to feelings of inadequacy by hurling putdowns at the spouse. Employees satisfy their irritation at a condescending supervisor by maintaining an "I-know-better" attitude among fellow workers. Parents often overuse their authority by inhibiting their children's personal growth, harshly stating the "right" decisions.

■ ■ ■ ▪

What tendencies give you an upper hand over someone in your life? *(For instance, I don't admit my flaws to my wife, although I will point out hers.)*

1. _____

_____

_____

2. _____

_____

_____

■ ■ ■ ▪

Trying to establish superiority provides temporary relief from inferior feelings, but it never succeeds in totally eliminating those lowly feelings. Instead, it is like riding a never-ending seesaw. You may be in the up position for a while, but your partner will eventually respond by putting you down. Then you try to elevate yourself again, and the game goes on and on. This adversarial edge in your relationships perpetuates ongoing anger.

RECOGNIZING EQUALITY

To avoid the inferior-superior trap, we must acknowledge that we are all equal in human value. As simple as this concept seems, it is hard to grasp because we resist being grouped under a label perceived as "ordinary."

As Russ discussed these matters with Dr. Carter, he protested, "Are you telling me I'm on the same level as some guy who's a habitual criminal and has never amounted to anything in his life? I mean, this notion of equality may sound good in theory, but come on! It just doesn't match real life."

Dr. Carter answered, "Let's take your habitual criminal question, and I'll show you what I mean. I can't determine whether my human value is higher than the criminal's until I have faced all the obstacles he has faced. I didn't grow up with the same parents he did or with the same teachers or peers or social relationships. I don't have the same genetic makeup or inborn temperament. I can say, though, that if I had been burdened with the same influences in my life, I might have turned out just as he did. The point is, it's folly to try to compare our human values, because we don't have the same playing fields.

"Russ, we tend to base our judgments on very superficial criteria when, in fact, it's not that simple," Dr. Carter continued. "I do believe we can have skills and traits deemed inferior or superior. But essentially we are the same, equal in both our intrinsic worth and in our inclination toward imperfection."

■ ■ ■ ■

What inhibits you from acknowledging the basic equality between individuals? *(For instance, in my childhood I heard criticism about the way other families managed things, and this made me feel my family was somehow superior.)*

1. _____

_____

2. _____

_____

■ ■ ■ ■

The apostle Peter struggled with the assumption that he, as a Jew, was superior to any Gentile. Acts 10 records the story of how he was prompted to witness to Cornelius, a Roman. Peter was very reluctant, but he finally did what God compelled him to do. And upon seeing Cornelius's eagerness to embrace Christianity, he remarked, "In truth I perceive that God shows no partiality" (Acts 10:34). Peter gave up his arrogance and related equally with someone he had previously despised.

Check the following statements you would agree with.

☐ I have no right to speak harshly or condescendingly to anyone.

☐ Being different does not mean a person is better or worse than I am.

☐ If I must confront someone, I can do it with respect.

☐ Being in a position of authority does not give me greater worth than another person.

☐ No human has the capacity to make a truly accurate judgment over another.

☐ If someone chooses to judge me, I am under no obligation to receive his or her opinion as fact.

☐ I can enjoy my uniqueness without assuming it gives me an advantage over others.

☐ My standing before God is the only judgment that truly matters.

The more of these statements you can check, the easier it will be for you to get off the inferior-superior seesaw.

If we recognize our equality with one another, we can manage our anger quite differently. When we are emotionally prompted to preserve our worth, needs, or convictions, we will have no desire to gain an upper hand or insult the other person as a means of elevating ourselves. Our words will be evenly presented. We can be firm, yet considerate.

> If we recognize our equality with one another, we can manage our anger quite differently.

Reflecting his new mind-set of equality, Russ could make subtle adjustments in his communication to reduce the aggressive elements of his anger. Note the following examples:

- When his son was slow in doing his chores, Russ would calmly say, "I know this isn't your favorite thing to do. Just keep in mind that you can get on with your weekend activities as soon as you've completed your work here."

- When he was frustrated with his wife's use of money, he would say, "Since you and I have different spending habits we're going to need extra patience with each other as we talk about keeping a balanced budget. I'm willing to discuss this topic constructively."

- When his stepdaughters argued in his presence, he could say, "Don't count on pulling me into the fray. I want you two to work out this problem before bedtime, then we can discuss how to keep these arguments from happening so often."

"Dr. Carter, it's interesting to watch the reactions of my family as I speak to them as equals," Russ said at a later session. "Instead of turning our discussion into a game of one-upmanship, reason leads the way. I like it a lot better because I'm less volatile. And when I'm less volatile, they're more responsive."

"Your level of anger is a direct by-product of your guiding thoughts," Dr. Carter responded. "When you react to difficulties with the thought,

I've got to get the upper hand, you are declaring war. You're doing yourself no favors because this brings out the worst in your personality and in the other person. The key to healthy anger is to communicate it with respect. I'm encouraged that you are learning it well."

MINIMIZING EVALUATIONS

"Russ, I'm emphasizing a no-judgment style of thinking," said Dr. Carter. "To succeed in adjusting your communication, I'd like to suggest a subtlety you can learn to avoid. I want you to consider how often you evaluate others in your communication."

"I've never really given much thought to it," he responded. "By evaluations, do you mean comparisons?"

"That and more. How many times has someone commented on your performance, no matter how small, by saying it was good or excellent or perhaps below par? And how many times have you graded someone in the same way, evaluating how their performance meets your standards?"

Smiling, he replied, "Well, it happens all the time. I'm constantly talking to my kids about how well they are doing in school or how well they are behaving. And I know they have their own ideas about how well I'm doing as a father. An evaluation mind-set is a constant."

Think of the common aspects of living that receive our evaluations:

- A parent sees an A on his or her child's test and says, "You're doing great. This is outstanding."

- A husband says to his wife, "That was a great supper. Keep up the good work!"

- One employee complains to another, "John just doesn't get the job done. He's mediocre at best."

- You feel a surge of strong anger, even hate, then think, *I'm awful for feeling this way.*

- You neglect your devotion time at home and chide yourself, *Good Christians don't struggle like this.*

Human beings are obsessed with evaluative standings. In any arena, be it job performance, emotional management, social skills, or Christian living, we feel compelled to grade the performance. Our self-esteem then rises or falls based on the latest report card.

■ ■ ■ ■

In what areas do you find yourself being most evaluative? *(For instance, I give myself a grade on my social prowess; I emphasize excellence constantly with my kids.)*

1. _____

   _____

   _____

2. _____

   _____

   _____

3. _____

   _____

   _____

■ ■ ■ ■

You may ask, "But what does an emphasis on evaluation have to do with anger?" Implied in any evaluation, no matter how positive, is the covertly communicated threat, *You'd better keep up the high performance, or I'll be forced to tell you how bad you are.* A strong emphasis on evaluation coupled with the inevitable inability to be perfect leads head-on to frustration—and anger.

Dr. Carter asked Russ, "What was it like for you during your childhood when a parent or teacher graded you for your performance?"

"I can remember being very conscientious about that. On the outside I'd try to give every appearance that I was the best. It was important to hear the words 'You did good.'"

"But on the inside?"

"On the inside I became weary. I would hide my bad performances, or I'd lie about any negative feelings. I was reluctant to let anyone see the things that might elicit a poor grade."

"And the emotional fallout? How would this make you feel?"

"I'd be defensive, and I'd get mad if anyone insisted I was less than adequate."

"And I'm wondering if any of that defensiveness frustrated you."

"Absolutely. I can recall many times when I secretly wished my dad would get off my back and just accept me without the performance criteria. It's really frustrating to think you have to make the grade before you can be loved."

Common sense tells us we are worth more than the sum total of our evaluations. After all, we are human beings, not human *doings*. But our proclivity toward judgment is so great we do not allow ourselves to be who we are. The apostle Paul explained to the Corinthians that

> But they, measuring themselves by themselves, and comparing themselves among themselves, are not wise.
> —2 Corinthians 10:12

any attempt to grade one another wasted energy. He wrote, "But they, measuring themselves by themselves, and comparing themselves among themselves, are not wise" (2 Corinthians 10:12). Humans create serious problems when we overemphasize grades and achievements. That is why we are instructed by God to stay out of the judgment business.

■ ■ ■ ■

Can you recall a time when you were unfairly judged by someone? (*For instance, when I went through a depression, I was told it was because I didn't have enough faith.*)

1. _____

_____

_____

2. _____

_____

_____

■ ■ ■ ■

To minimize your struggles with anger, step back from the grades and judgments of others. Recognize that no evaluation is perfectly given. Instead, learn to be descriptive in your thoughts.

Dr. Carter told Russ, "You would save yourself a lot of irritation if you exchanged your grades for descriptions."

"What do you mean?"

"For instance, when you discuss school work with your teenagers, instead of saying, 'You did a great job,' describe what must be going on inside. Tell them, 'When you've studied hard for an exam and it turns out well, it gives you great satisfaction, doesn't it?' It's what I call talking to the insides of a person."

"That would be entirely different from what I do now. I'm not sure I could do it."

"Sure you can," replied Dr. Carter. "It will require some creativity, but it can be done. You can turn your thoughts toward a person's feelings rather than what he or she has done. It's a very rewarding style of communicating.

"Also," continued Dr. Carter, "you can learn to sidestep the judgments applied to you by others. If someone tells you how great you did on a project, don't become enamored by the evaluation; the next day that person may tell you how lousy you've performed on something else. Accept feedback and be willing to learn, but don't let your emotional stability hang on the latest evaluation."

After Russ took a personal inventory of his tendency to evaluate, he made the following adjustments:

   When his son made a D on a math test, Russ said, "I know you were disappointed when you saw this grade. It gives you a sinking feeling inside, doesn't it?"

- When dinner was ready, he told his wife, "You were really busy this afternoon yet you found time to get the meal together. I sure appreciate your dedication!"

- When he felt a surge of strong anger, rather than condemning himself for having the emotion, he thought, *I'm feeling more tense today than normal; that tells me I need to take time to relax.*

- If he had lapses in his daily devotions, he would remind himself, *I know there are times when I feel distant from God, but that does not mean I'm supposed to respond inwardly with self-condemnation.*

When we apply descriptive thinking, we remember that we do not have Godlike abilities to properly judge. Therefore, we can continue to express helpful ideas or perceptions, but without the emotional baggage of false guilt or self-directed anger.

■ ■ ■ ■

How could you exchange evaluative thoughts for descriptions? *(For instance, I would refrain from being critical toward my family, focusing instead on why they feel as they do; I would worry less about my comparative standing with others.)*

1. _____

_____

_____

2. _____

_____

_____

3. _____

_____

_____

■ ■ ■ ■

Sidestepping human evaluations keeps us from being aggressive and competitive. Rather than getting lured into false games of superiority, we are more capable of seeing people for what they are: fellow sinners who have an equal need for God's grace.

Part Four

Applying
New Insights about
Anger Reduction

11

▪▪ Managing a Child's Anger

▪ ## Step 11. Pass along to the next generation your insights about anger.

Ideally, healthy anger management is learned during childhood and refined as the stages of life unfold. Unfortunately, most parents were not properly guided in using anger during their own childhoods, and their accumulated bad habits are then passed along to the next generation. It can be an ever-perpetuating cycle until someone steps forward and says, "The buck stops here."

One such person was Patricia. When she came for counseling, she was in her early forties, the mother of a fifteen-year-old boy and a ten-year-old girl. She had sought help because her emotions were ruling her life. She admitted she was causing so much tension, her family was coming apart.

In an early visit with Dr. Carter she said, "Either I get a grip on my tension or I'm going to lose my husband. And if that happens, my children will surely turn against me. They're tired of my constant irritability."

She began a series of counseling sessions that trained her to minimize her emotional ups and downs. After incorporating the insights she had learned and significantly reducing her level of anger, she stated, "I don't want my children to enter adulthood with the same baggage I had. Starting now I want to give them some tips about handling their emotions successfully. Jason is fifteen, so I don't have a lot of time left with him, but I know he would be receptive. Jennifer is ten, and she's just like I was at that age, sweet in public but sour in private."

"By reflecting on your own childhood experiences perhaps you can remember what it's like to be their ages, having emotions but not feeling certain what to do with them," Dr. Carter suggested.

"Oh, I know what they are going through. They've seen me on my emotional roller coaster often enough to be confused. Sometimes they bottle up their frustrations, which become seeds for discontent and resentment. Other times they jump right in and slug it out."

"Are they openly argumentative with you?"

"Sometimes they are. Jason wants to be very independent, so he usually resists restrictions I put on him. He has a real temper when pushed. Jennifer is more of a pouter and whiner. When she's angry, she becomes cranky. She really knows how to push my buttons."

"It's going to require some consistency and discipline on your part," said Dr. Carter, "but with persistence you can become the guide they need."

Patricia's attitude was to be commended. It is good for adults to improve their own anger skills, since the generations behind us are carefully observing the modeling we offer. These days, kids live in a world that offers many reasons to feel angry. How skillfully do you communicate with your children as you teach them to sift out their choices in managing anger? If the youth in your world were to base their management of anger upon the behaviors and attitudes you demonstrate, how well off would they be?

Look over the following incidences to get an idea of ways children might mismanage anger based on what they see in an adult. For instance:

- A dad has been kicked off of his daughter's soccer field twice in one season for yelling unmercifully at the fifteen-year-old umpires.

A single mom knows that her thirteen-year-old doesn't like her partying with her friends until late hours in their backyard on weekends, yet she does it anyway.

Parents have had loud arguments, exchanging curse words and throwing objects, yet they wonder why their son has been reprimanded at school for being disruptive.

A teen does not meet the criteria for a solo in the school play, and her frustration is made worse by her parent who won't stop complaining to the school officials.

A parent purchases violent video games for his son and plays with him, cheering each time he makes a kill.

Criticism abounds in the home, leaving the child feeling that nothing can be done to please.

■ ■ ■ ■

Surely you are aware of the phrase, "Actions speak louder than words." As you examine the influence you have on the young people in your life, what tendencies would you need to give up in order to improve your modeling? *(For instance, There is no real need for me to yell when I am disciplining; I tell my child to show respect toward others, yet I know she is aware of my deep bitterness toward my ex.)*

1. _____

   _____

   _____

2. _____

   _____

   _____

3. _____

   _____

   _____

◼ KEYS TO HANDLING YOUR CHILD'S ANGER

Perhaps the greatest error parents make is letting the child set the agenda for how emotions are managed in the family. Parents may have good intentions about being firm or fair-minded, but when the child fails to respond as expected those good intentions go right out the window. This is what we call a reactor mentality in the parent. To counter this tendency, parents need to go on the initiative. Rather than wondering, *How can I get the child to behave so I can be composed?* they can ask themselves, *How can I be composed so I can get the child to behave?*

There are several ways to accomplish this. In this chapter we'll share six ideas we've found to be effective: (1) don't be threatened by your child's anger, (2) let choices and consequences shape the child, (3) don't preach, (4) don't major on the minors (meaning don't let minor problems deplete your parenting energy supply), (5) share your own experiences, and (6) incorporate spiritual insights delicately. Let's look at each of these suggestions separately.

Don't Be Threatened by Your Child's Anger

In Chapter 8 we examined how anger can be caused by unresolved fears that are manifested as defensiveness. Do you ever think of yourself as being *afraid* of your child's anger? If you get easily caught in power plays, or if you often speak tensely to your child, you may be exhibiting this kind of defensiveness and revealing how threatened you are. It is important to recognize that an overpowering form of communication does not represent strength—it indicates that you feel inadequate. Inevitably the child will react with manipulation.

Dr. Carter sensed that Patricia worried too much about her son's responses to her discipline. "When Jason balks at your discipline, it seems to spark a tense reaction in you. It's as though you're thinking, *How dare he disagree with my wisdom!*"

"Well, in a sense that's exactly what I'm thinking," she replied. "I can't figure out why he has to be so contrary. For example, last Saturday he wanted to spend the entire day with his friends, then go again that evening. I made him stay home in the afternoon to finish some chores. By his reaction you would have thought I was the Wicked Witch of the West. I don't know what to do when he gets into these moods, but they have got to stop."

"I can appreciate the annoyance you felt," said Dr. Carter, "but let's look at something very basic. Kids Jason's age want to be with their peers. In fact, it would be abnormal if he didn't want to hang out with his buddies. So when Mom says he needs to stay home, he's going to interpret that as a real insult. Now you and I both know you have sound reasons for your decision, but he hasn't taken the time to consider your viewpoint. And he probably won't consider your viewpoint deeply for many years to come. So it's no surprise he would balk."

"You're saying I am too easily shocked by his anger when I really should just accept it as a normal teenage reaction?"

"That's right. Children have an ongoing internal conflict about authority. At one level they know they need the guidance, but on another level they're preoccupied with themselves and they want zero input. So his response is hardly surprising. He's playing out his conflict with you.

"My suggestion is," Dr. Carter continued, "don't be threatened by his anger. He's just being normal. This doesn't mean you shouldn't maintain your boundaries. But don't feel like you have to immediately squelch his irritation. That's not your job."

Parents who are easily threatened by a child's anger respond in several common ways. Check the following responses that apply to you.

- ☐ You say yes when you know it is best to say no.
- ☐ When a child challenges your ideas, you immediately speak with greater force.
- ☐ You give excessive explanations for choosing a discipline.
- ☐ Inwardly you think, *How dare my child speak to me in that tone of voice.*
- ☐ You are not sure your child takes you seriously when you say something.
- ☐ Discussions with your child can feel like a battle of wills.
- ☐ You will fume for quite a while after a confrontation with your child.
- ☐ You give in too easily to a child's whining or fussing, wanting peace at any cost.

■ ■ ■ ■ ▪

What are some examples of times you have been threatened by your child's anger? *(For instance, I responded very heavy-handedly when my daughter talked back to me.)*

1. _____

_____

_____

2. _____

_____

_____

■ ■ ■ ■ ▪

When we respond in fear to a child's anger, we communicate, *You are a very powerful force in my life, and I have to overwhelm you to teach you anything.* It is an invitation to battle. And any time a parent battles the child, everyone loses.

So what is the alternative? First, let your child be human. You've had moments of irritability, too, and you probably don't respond all that well when someone attempts to scold you for your emotions. Allow your child the same latitude. Second, quietly hold firm to your rightful authority, even if the child eyes you with skepticism or contempt. If your words make sense and your discipline is fair, let them stand on their own merits. Don't attempt to sell a child something that needs no salesmanship.

> If your words make sense and your discipline is fair, let them stand on their own merits.

When you lose your shock over a child's anger, the result is increased objectivity and the ability to relate with reason and fairness. Stability and logic, rather than knee-jerk emotion, will be your guide. A calm firmness will permeate your character, prompting the child to realize the futility of power plays.

Dr. Carter explained to Patricia, "When you are not threatened by your child's anger, you can use the 'nonetheless' approach to discipline."

She smiled as she responded, "I'm not sure what you mean by the 'nonetheless' approach, but I'm all ears."

"Suppose you tell your son, 'If you are going out with your friends tonight, I'll need you to stay home this afternoon to help me clean the garage.' He protests angrily and complains how unreasonable you are for making him do slave's labor."

"Have you been looking in my windows? That sounds just like some of the conversations we have," Patricia said.

"At that point you are susceptible to being threatened by his anger, and you feel compelled to defend your decision by explaining why he should not be feeling as he does."

"I do that all the time, but it never seems to get me anywhere."

"Patricia, your explanations only fuel his fire. So it's time to drop them in favor of a 'nonetheless' statement. You can say, 'Jason, I know you're frustrated because you'll have to alter your plans. Nonetheless, the garage needs to be cleaned this afternoon.'"

"But Dr. Carter, what if he continues to protest? He's not going to just fall in line based on one calm statement I make."

"Don't be threatened by his protest. Continue your course. You can say again, 'Nonetheless the garage needs to be cleaned so you can go out this evening.' And if he protests again, tell him the same thing again with no pleading or persuasion. It's your way of communicating that you are confident enough in your decision that you can withstand his angry reaction. Eventually he'll get the picture and lower his anger level."

■ ■ ■ ■

As you consider being more confident in yourself and less threatened by your child's emotions, what adjustments could you make when your child responds irritably to you? *(For instance, when my daughter complains about her supper, I can calmly tell her, "I know you're disappointed because this is not what you were hoping for tonight; nonetheless, this is what we're having for supper, and this is what you get to eat.")*

1. _____

   _____

   _____

2. _____

   _____

   _____

■ ■ ■ ■

By recommending that you drop your sense of shock and be less defensive about your decisions, we are not suggesting that you never explain your reasoning to the child. Sometimes it can be quite helpful for the child to know why you make the decisions you do. But if your explanations rapidly deteriorate into a useless debate, it is time to hold your ground with calm firmness even if the child remains in a frustrated frame of mind. The unexaggerated confidence you exude sets the pace for a fair-minded emotional exchange.

Let Choices and Consequences Shape the Child

We parents can be impatient for children to learn important lessons. For example, if a child is rude or disruptive to a sibling, we want the child to stop behaving so intolerably. So what do we do? We tell the child how to think. We give lectures and follow up with threats. And how does this affect the child? He or she becomes angrier and inwardly vows that no one will tell him or her what to do. It is not the instruction itself that the child is angry about, it is the fact that the adult is not letting the child have choices.

In one of her early counseling sessions with Dr. Carter, Patricia revealed how she typically succumbed to ineffective responses when her ten-year-old daughter Jennifer would whine about something trivial. For example, Jennifer commonly griped about not having enough clothes to wear or not having anything to do to fill her free time. Patricia's typical response would be, "How can you possibly think those things? Your closet is full of clothes, and the cabinet has more games in it than you'll ever play! You can't say you've got it bad."

Dr. Carter responded with a smile and a sly question, "When you say that to Jennifer, how many times does she reply with, 'Hey, Mom, thanks for pointing that out, I guess I needed the perspective'?"

Laughing, Patricia said, "Never! We just get drawn further into a hole of anger."

"Your mistake," said Dr. Carter, "is trying to think for your daughter. Rather than doing the mental work for her, let her choose for herself how she'll handle her tension. For example, when she says she has nothing to wear to school, let her know she can select whatever is in her closet. Then be quiet and allow her choices to unfold."

"But if I tell her that, she might make a poor choice. I'm not going to let her go to school looking totally inappropriate."

"I can appreciate your concern," said Dr. Carter, "although I caution you against being too finicky about the choices you'll allow. My point is that you are doing her no favors by trying to think for her. She needs the experience of struggling with her own emotions. Right now her decisions are relatively harmless, but ten years from now when she is living on her own, she'll need to know how to sift through opinions about more complex matters and make the best choice. Now is the best time for her to develop strategies for managing her emotions. But she won't become proficient if you get in the way."

■ ■ ■ ■

What are some common situations when you try to think for your child and steer his or her emotions your way? (*For instance, when my son complains that his friends are mean, I tell him to quit worrying about it and play with someone else.*)

1. _____

_____

_____

2. _____

_____

_____

■ ■ ■ ■

Children need to feel competent to manage their own anger. With that in mind, parents can toss the ball into their court by asking questions such as, "What do you think can be done about this?" or "What opinions do you have?" In this subtle way, the parent communicates confidence in the child.

"Let's take a common situation," suggested Dr. Carter, "and I'll show you what I mean. Let's assume Jennifer complains that her brother is rude to her. She comes whining to you about the problem, prompting you to grope for ways to solve their tension. Is that a fairly common scenario in your home?"

"All too common. Jennifer can really make life miserable when Jason puts her in a foul mood."

"It's at times like this when you'll be tempted to think for Jennifer. So let's be careful about deciding how you'll respond. Normally, you might say, 'Well, just stay away from Jason and quit fighting.' Right?"

"Right. It doesn't usually work, but you've got me pegged."

"Well, let's try a different approach, one that encourages Jennifer to take greater responsibility for her emotions. Throw the problem back into her lap by telling her, 'I see you're feeling frustrated because Jason shows you no respect. What options do you have to manage this frustration?'"

"Dr. Carter, she'll probably continue whining and say, 'I don't know.'"

"Don't take her bait; instead, tell her, 'This won't be an easy problem to solve, but you always have choices. You can argue back with Jason, you can hold a grudge, or you can go to a different part of the house. Which choice makes the most sense to you?' Keep putting it back into her lap."

"What if she chooses to go back to Jason and scream?"

"Let her know that is, indeed, an option, but it carries a consequence, perhaps no play time for the rest of the afternoon. She'll soon learn to pick a different option."

■ ■ ■ ■

In what areas could you more freely offer choices to your children? *(For instance, I could let them choose the time of day they complete their homework assignments.)*

1. _____

   _____

   _____

2. _____

   _____

   _____

3. _____

   _____

   _____

■ ■ ■ ■ ▪

Using choices and consequences can be more time-consuming for parents than merely telling the child what to do. But the child becomes more responsible and is forced to think about the direction of his or her emotions. It causes the child to struggle to come to terms with who he or she will be. Ultimately, the child becomes an initiator of healthy behavior rather than just one who lives according to someone else's dogma.

Don't Preach

To teach our children to handle their anger correctly, we adults must model healthy communication. That means avoiding such ironic responses to a child's anger as warning, "You'd better get your act together or I'll give you something to be mad about." The irony is the condescending anger this adult shows while he or she tells the child to stop being angry. The child responds more to the tone of the message than to the message itself.

> Adults are more effective in helping children handle their anger when they give a low-key performance in the authority figure role.

Adults are more effective in helping children handle their anger when they give a low-key performance in the authority figure role. To put it another way, the top dog who barks too loudly is ultimately regarded as an insecure nuisance.

To determine if you lean too heavily on an authoritative style, check the level of persuasion in your speech. Do you debate fine points with your child? Do you offer rebuttals to your child's point of view? Do you work extra hard to convince the child of the validity of your opinion? Do you accuse your child of insubordination and induce guilt for being different? Is your tone of voice harsh or controlling?

■ ■ ■ ■

In what ways do you carry out the authority figure role too heavy-handedly? *(For instance, I raise my voice when my child disagrees with me; I make too many threats.)*

1. _____

_____

_____

2. _____

_____

_____

3. _____

_____

_____

■ ■ ■ ■

Patricia admitted, "I know I'm less effective with my kids when I'm heavy-handed; it only increases their anger. But it's hard to resist the temptation to come on strong when one of them is contrary."

"From personal experience, I know that to be true," Dr. Carter nodded. "But I want you to focus on a subtle but powerful truth: Our greatest impact on people is not in the words we speak but in the way we deliver those words. Our manner can convey many unspoken messages about our respect and trust for the other person and about our confidence in ourselves. When we speak too strongly, it implies disrespect, lack of trust, and personal insecurity."

"You're implying then that I should respond to my kids' anger with an even tone of voice. That's easier said than done."

"That's so true," Dr. Carter replied. "But if you can keep an even tone, you are showing your children how to disagree without being disagreeable. You are showing them that differentness does not have to result in an adversarial relationship. You would also illustrate that you have decided in advance that you want to model healthy conflict resolution."

Learn to recognize the meaning of your child's anger. Recall in Chapter 1 how we explored anger's link to self-preservation instincts. When you speak to a child in a way that emphasizes your authority over his or her worth, you keep the anger alive in that child. But when you speak respectfully, even in disagreements, you diffuse the reason for the anger.

Don't Major in the Minors

Have you noticed how children get upset over the most trivial things?

- An eight-year-old girl is mad because her mother makes her wear pants on a cold day rather than the skirt she prefers.

- A fifteen-year-old boy complains that he has to be home at night thirty minutes earlier than his buddy.

- A group of fifth-graders moan about the extra math homework the teacher assigned.

- A teenager thinks it is unreasonable to place limits on time spent on the computer or a gaming station.

- An eager young boy pouts because his mother won't let him ride his bike on a stormy afternoon.

Children are not faced with the same issues that confront their parents. Their big dilemmas are small in comparison to worries about inflation, health care, rising crime, etc. Nonetheless, it is necessary for them to resolve the problems that seem major. They feel just as irritated about an insult on the school playground as we feel about business matters that cause financial strain. And their maturity is slowed when adults don't know how to respond to their emotions.

In most cases, when minor problems affect our children, we parents make the mistake of giving them too much attention. In doing so, we increase the child's anger. For example:

- When an eleven-year-old girl says she wants to buy an item that costs three dollars more than her mother wants to spend, the mother reacts with extreme agitation and put-downs.

- When a sixteen-year-old son forgets to fill the car with gas as his dad requested, the father grounds him for two weeks.

- When a seven-year-old spills a drink on the kitchen floor, the parent complains repeatedly about the child's clumsiness, warning it cannot be tolerated.

Sound absurd? It is. But too often we expend excessive energy on issues of little significance, thus perpetuating an atmosphere of unnecessary anger.

■ ■ ■ ■

When have you have majored on the minors? *(For instance, I gave my son the silent treatment for several hours when he told me he forgot to bring a book home from school.)*

1. _____

_____

_____

2. _____

_____

_____

3. _____

_____

_____

■ ■ ■ ■

Why do we do this? Our overemphasis on trivial things represents a shallow understanding of the purpose of relationships. When we respond this way, the important matters of relationships—respect, encouragement, and empathy—take a backseat to perfectionism, selfishness, impatience, and petty preferences.

Check the following statements you can agree with.

☐ I'd rather let a child make minor errors and learn from those mistakes than insist on a mistake-free life.

☐ In our home, differentness is not only allowed, it is often encouraged. I prefer to save my discipline for issues that really matter.

☐ When a child becomes upset over simple things, I can be objective and not get pulled into the emotions of the moment.

☐ When my child is intent on griping, I need to model what a rational attitude looks like.

☐ I can chuckle or smile to myself about some of the little worries that bother kids.

☐ I am not obligated to fix every minor problem my child presents to me.

When we focus too heavily on minor issues, we teach children to be imbalanced in their anger. But when we let minor issues remain minor, the emotions are minimized.

Share Your Own Experiences

Children are at a disadvantage because they are not as aware of adult struggles as we are of their problems. When they become angry or insecure, their emotions are on display for all the world to see. But when adults become angry or insecure, those feelings are often hidden. Or worse, children easily see the adult's emotion but they are not allowed to discuss their reactions to it. This leaves the child with a negative feeling of differentness that ultimately increases irritability.

Children need openness and honesty with their parents if they are to develop emotional composure, and this openness should not be a one-way window into the child's feelings. Children need to see the insides of their parents too.

Patricia raised an eyebrow when Dr. Carter suggested that openness with Jason and Jennifer would go a long way toward helping them contain their emotions. "I'm not sure it would be best to confess my problems to my children. For their own security they need to think I've got it together."

"Let's look at an interesting idea," Dr. Carter responded. "Your children are insightful enough to know you have mood swings just as they do. But it creates more questions than it solves when you are secretive about them. You'll show your level of inner confidence when you can freely discuss your own emotions with them. You'll become more believable and thus more approachable. Ultimately this removes the pressure for them to be perfect, and their own emotions are less severe."

The next week she reported, "I tried what we discussed and was amazed at the result. Jennifer was complaining about being rejected by a friend at school, and I shared with her a similar experience I had when I was her age. As I told her my story her mood shifted noticeably. She was more relaxed, and several times in the next couple of days she asked follow-up questions."

"So when you shared with her, she felt less isolated," said Dr. Carter. "Your self-disclosure created an opportunity for cohesion. I imagine her pain then became less severe."

■ ■ ■ ■

What keeps you from being open in your parent-child communications? (*For instance, my parents never spoke about personal matters with me; I stay too focused on performances.*)

1. _____

_____

_____

2. _____

_____

_____

3. _____

_____

_____

■ ■ ■ ■

When parents refuse to be vulnerable with their children, they create an atmosphere of phoniness and false superiority, and the children resent it. Ultimately, the parents' authority position is weakened. But when parents are willing to be authentic, family communication opens significantly. The child thinks, *Hey, you really do know what the score is. I can relate to you now.*

Think of a time in your own experiences when a friend or relative made himself or herself vulnerable and shared a very personal matter with you. Were you put off by it? Were you offended? Or were you appreciative? Did your respect for that person increase? If managed appropriately, that relationship was probably strengthened substantially, much as it would be if you injected deep sharing into your relationship with your child.

■ ■ ■ ■

Respond to the following sentences.

When I tell my child of a struggle similar to his, he is likely to feel

_____

If I refuse to expose my humanness to my child, our relationship will probably _____

_____

The reward for self-disclosure would be _____

_____

■ ■ ■ ■

Incorporate Spiritual Insights Delicately

Anger management is ultimately a function of spiritual maturity. When we are in a right relationship with God, living consistently in His plans, we find the strength to overcome adversities that might otherwise seem paralyzing. The prophet Isaiah explained, "You will keep him in perfect peace, whose mind is stayed on You" (Isaiah 26:3).

Spiritual insights are necessary for each child who seeks emotional peace. But how well are these insights taught? Most children's exposure to spiritual life consists of hearing interesting Bible stories and learning a long list of do's and dont's. That's it. But beyond the objective facts, they need guidance to incorporate solid, practical truths into their daily lives. The process of teaching spiritual insights to a child is not complex, but it requires great delicacy. That is, truths about grace or forgiveness or respectful confrontation can be woven into everyday communication as common circumstances arise.

> You will keep him in perfect peace, whose mind is stayed on You.
> —Isaiah 26:3

■ ■ ■ ■

What are some of the prominent spiritual truths you want your child to incorporate? *(For instance, I want my child to know the merits of forgiveness; I want my child to be less self-serving and more sensitive to others.)*

1. _____

_____

2. _____

_____

3. _____

_____

4. _____

_____

■ ■ ■ ■

Now ask yourself, *How do I go about teaching these truths to my child?*

Patricia was particularly eager to pass along good spiritual instructions to her children. She told Dr. Carter, "I guess I've lectured my kids dozens of times about the advantages of spiritual commitments. They both have a reasonable understanding of the basics, but I'm not sure they understand how those spiritual truths can guide them in daily matters."

"Let me hazard a guess that you usually tell Jason and Jennifer what truths they should know without asking their opinion about how to make them relevant."

"I've never thought about it much, but I think you're right. So what are you getting at?"

"Once the children have been taught the basic rules of right and wrong," Dr. Carter explained, "your role can shift from instructor to facilitator. Take common situations and ask them to apply spiritual values to those situations."

Here are examples of how Patricia learned to communicate in deeper ways:

- Jason was aware that some of his friends had experimented with alcohol, so Patricia mentioned, "You've heard me talk about maintaining a good witness for the Lord, but I'm curious to know how you feel about it when you are with these friends."

- When Jennifer expressed anger toward a friend who had been rude, Patricia asked, "Do you suppose you can forgive even when a friend does nothing to deserve it?"

Children will not always apply spiritual truths maturely. They can be wildly erratic (as adults can) in remembering what they've learned. The parents' goal is not to force spiritual perfection but to keep contemplative thinking alive. In time, children can fine-tune their religious concepts as they gain understanding of God's plan for their lives. By encouraging inquisitiveness about biblical truths, their beliefs are less legalistic and more personally meaningful.

Patricia smiled as she and Dr. Carter discussed insights about anger in her dealings with her children. "I guess you can say that my modeling would fall under the category of 'easier said than done.' This really requires concentration on a moment by moment basis."

Certainly Patricia's sentiments were right on target, but who else is going to step up and demonstrate emotional maturity if not you? Their siblings? Classmates? Television idols? Let's hope that you will consider it a privilege and responsibility to set the pace as your life habits demonstrate that you are a person who is in a constant growth mode.

12

:: Why Anger Lingers

■ **Step 12. Avoid the temptation to rationalize your anger; assume full responsibility for who you are.**

"Dr. Minirth, you just don't seem to understand. I know I've got a lot of anger to overcome, but my situation doesn't fit very neatly into your therapeutic formulas. I'm not sure I can just flip a switch in my mind and suddenly let go of the rage I feel."

Mike was an overweight man in his late twenties. He had spent five years working as an engineer for a large corporation but had been laid off during a buyout of the company. The timing of his layoff was seemingly a blessing because he was suffering burnout anyway. But six months had passed, and he had yet to schedule a single interview for a new job. He was married with no children, and he admitted uncertainty about ever starting a family. He would ask, "With all the misery in my life, why should I make things more complicated by having kids?"

Mike's history was not good. His parents had endured a violent relationship that had included verbal abuse, shoving, and cursing. Predictably, when they were angry with each other, one or both would displace their frustration on Mike and his older sister. "I've been cursed at so many times that I couldn't possibly count them. I was especially afraid of my dad because he would beat me unmercifully if I strayed from his rules. He was a control freak; he would lose it if I ever disagreed with him. My mother wasn't much better in containing her anger, but at least she didn't beat me like my dad did."

During his teen years Mike became increasingly volatile in his own angry expressions. He was active in sports and was known as the most aggressive kid around. He took delight in his tough guy reputation. He had married at age twenty-four, but never had good rapport with his wife, Charlotte. She told Dr. Minirth, "It's like he's reenacting his father's life, but without the physical abuse, at least so far. Sometimes I am afraid he might hit me. We're not very close to each other. Our marriage is real work."

After four months of therapy Mike showed little real improvement in his anger management. He was diagnosed with bipolar disorder and properly medicated, which curbed some of his extreme expressions. He had gone for longer spells without screaming at Charlotte, but it was more of a forced adjustment than a true choice. Internally, he was just as easily provoked by minor matters as he had always been.

Dr. Minirth addressed Mike's ongoing anger in a very forthright way. "Mike, you've been learning a lot about yourself, but it's leading nowhere. That tells me your commitment to change is suspect. You say you would like to be free of your unhealthy emotions, but I'm not really sure you mean it."

"I do mean it," Mike protested. "Why would I deliberately choose to stay angry? I don't need that kind of life. It's just that my problems are so big I can't kick myself into gear."

Undaunted, Dr. Minirth responded, "I've worked with countless others who could match your horror stories, yet they've chosen not to remain imprisoned by their emotions. They've changed, and so can you. Your primary task right now is to let go of any excuses that keep you tied to your unhealthy anger."

RATIONALIZATIONS THAT PERPETUATE ANGER

When we cling to anger in spite of potentially helpful knowledge and insights, it is usually due to an intricate system of rationalization. Change is difficult. It requires up-to-the-minute self-awareness, persistent effort, and a stubborn willingness to restructure the thoughts and perceptions that guide us. But we humans can be lazy. We want to change, but we resist the notion of hard work. Therefore if changes required in anger management do not come easily, we may shun personal responsibility by hiding behind rationalizations. Instead of admitting, *I choose to cling to my anger,* we prefer to think, *My anger is in me because of someone else's problems.*

■ ■ ■ ■

Be as honest as you can with yourself. What excuses do you hide behind to justify your ongoing unhealthy anger? *(For instance, my spouse never cooperates with me; my father never loved me.)*

1. _____

_____

_____

2. _____

_____

_____

3. _____

_____

_____

■ ■ ■ ■

Most of our rationalizations are seductive because they contain an element of truth. So we cling to that truth while "forgetting" we can go a different route. For example, Mike did indeed have a reason to be angry about his parents' abuse. No child should ever have to endure what he endured. But instead of deciding as an adult that he would be healthy, he rationalized his anger by thinking, *I've been denied a fair hearing all my life, so I'm not about to let my current world roll over me.*

You can determine if you are rationalizing your anger by asking the following questions:

- Do I express my anger aggressively in spite of my good intentions to be properly assertive?

- Are my episodes of inappropriate anger a repeat of earlier, similar incidents?

- Do I have a feeling the world owes me more than it is willing to give?

- Do I blame God for my problems, cynically questioning why He won't spare me from my miseries?

- Have I become insensitive to the way my anger affects the well-being of other people?

- Have I given up hope that I can be a consistently balanced person?

If you answered yes to any of the above questions, you are susceptible to excusing yourself from being responsible for your emotional well-being.

> **To effectively manage your anger, you will need to set aside your rationalizations and decide to thrive with God's guidance.**

To effectively manage your anger, you will need to set aside your rationalizations and decide to thrive with God's guidance. Below, several of the most common excuses are exposed.

My past is too painful.

We all are influenced by our environments. Each of us has a God-given reactor mode that causes us to be highly attuned to the emotional atmosphere around us. For instance, people who are regularly exposed to loving interchanges are more naturally inclined to respond in kind. Likewise, people who live in a tension-filled environment respond with defensiveness.

When we counsel persons with longstanding anger problems, invariably we uncover an emotional history full of pain. Most commonly, angry people recall the indignity of enduring a parent's foul temper. And often these same people have similarly painful experiences in their adult lives with spouses, relatives, or close friends. After years of feeling attacked and bruised, futility settles in, causing a pessimistic "what's-the-use?" mind-set to guide the emotions. That's what had happened to Mike.

Modern psychotherapy has trained many suffering people to believe they cannot come to terms with their current anger until they have "worked through" the pain of the past. In this therapy, anger must be admitted and reexperienced so the sufferers can gain a new perspective and then move forward with proper adjustments. While it is indeed necessary in most cases to understand the beginnings of angry emotional patterns, many people allow themselves to become so obsessed with the past it becomes larger than current life. It is possible to be too historically oriented.

Throughout his twenties, Mike could hardly enjoy his adulthood because he continually recalled how his history affected his present life. For example, if he had a disagreement with a supervisor, he would think, *My dad was always unreasonable, and now I have to live with this.* Or if his wife forgot to do a favor he had asked, he would say, "You're just like my mother, all promises but no delivery." Experiences that occurred fifteen or more years ago were as fresh to him as if they had occurred the day before. If his wife asked him to stop comparing her with his painful past, he would protest by saying, "It's easy for you to tell me to give it up, but how can I when it is so real to me?"

■ ■ ■ ■

What past pain do you allow to affect your current emotions? *(For instance, my father was impossible to talk to, so I keep my distance from any male authority figure.)*

1. _____

_____

_____

2. _____

_____

_____

3. _____

_____

_____

■ ■ ■ ■

Why do we struggle to let go of past pain? Why do we allow it to perpetually revisit us many years later? We like control. Or, more strongly stated, we *crave* control. We cannot tolerate the notion that people can and will operate outside the realm of our wishes. When we cling to a rationalization such as *My past is too painful,* we are really thinking, *I can't be satisfied until I find an authoritative way to squelch those wrong experiences.*

To get beyond a painful past we must humbly acknowledge our inability to control others, particularly when the experiences are irretrievable. This requires us to accept a difficult notion: pain is inevitable and sometimes almost unbearable. Furthermore, it cannot be fully controlled or eliminated.

Mike said quietly to Dr. Minirth, "I hate to think I've got to just accept the fact that my parents inflicted pain on me and there's nothing I can do about it."

Dr. Minirth had already assisted Mike in writing letters to his parents. He also had role-modeled conversations with them and helped Mike find new ways to speak with them from a position of equality. He was also aware that these efforts had made little impact. Mike's parents apologized for nothing and made few, if any, adjustments in their ongoing relationship with him.

"Mike, I know it seems unfair to think you've attempted to correct your relationship with your parents but to no avail," he said during one session. "It makes the pain and anger feel all the more intense, doesn't it?"

Tears welled up as Mike replied, "Why does this misery have to go on? Why does it have to hurt so much? Why can't I just move forward without worrying about what they've done?"

"You *can* move forward. But to do so, you'll have to drop the idea that things can be fair. Your mom and dad weren't fair years ago, and it appears unlikely they will change any time soon. I'm thinking now, though, about what is most profitable for you rather that what is fair. It would be profitable for you to acknowledge that you cannot control the past, but you *can* choose a new direction for yourself."

Dr. Minirth then explained that letting go of the desire to control the past would require certain adjustments:

- When Mike's parents would speak condescendingly to him, he would choose not to respond in his old defensively angry manner rather than grumbling about how this is a continuance of an old nuisance.

- If his wife was in a bad mood, he would remember that she is not exactly like his mother, and he would refrain from scolding her for having normal human imperfections.

- If a coworker was too authoritarian in his or her speech, he was under no obligation to enter a power play as he often did with his father. He could remind himself that while it was impossible to control that coworker, he could choose to pursue his work in a sensible manner.

■ ■ ■ ■

If you more readily accepted the reality of past pain, what adjustments would you make in your current relationships? *(For instance, I would let my husband love me in his own way rather than demanding that he read my mind and cater to my controlling desires.)*

1. _____

_____

_____

2. _____

_____

_____

3. _____

_____

_____

■ ■ ■ ■

Dr. Minirth gave Mike an analogy. "You've participated in sports, so you appreciate how injuries can affect an athlete's play. I'm familiar with a coach who responds to a player's knee surgery by saying the player cannot return to team play until the knee is restored to 110 percent of its original strength. This coach reasons that the injury can motivate the athlete to become even stronger than before. In the same way, you can respond to your historical pain by being determined to seek a healthier way to manage your frustrations. Instead of letting the past hold you down, let it propel you to exciting, new growth."

Forgiveness Is Too Good

In Chapter 2 we examined how anger management sometimes consists of dropping the anger and choosing forgiveness instead. There are times, as Mike could attest, that all the textbook efforts to openly respond to frustrations fall short. So, rather than clinging to empty efforts, we can forgive.

But what happens when the person to be forgiven has done nothing to deserve that forgiveness? This was the question that haunted Mike as he tried to make sense of his parents' unhealthy behavior.

"Since my childhood Sunday school days, I've known we are supposed to forgive. But Dr. Minirth, if I choose to forgive, it seems I'm conceding defeat. And I'm not comfortable with that."

"So you cling to the anger because forgiveness seems to let others off the hook too easily. It seems like you're paying a very high price for another's unrepentant ways."

"But think about it! What father should be forgiven for beating his children and instilling fear in them every day? I feel like I'm being disloyal to my personal convictions if I forgive that."

"You're making a good point, one that is difficult to refute," replied Dr. Minirth. "I'd have a hard time, too, if I had been regularly exposed to such abuse. I guess this means we're going to have to carefully examine the motive that would help you forgive."

■ ■ ▪ ▫

What experiences in your life seem undeserving of forgiveness? (*For instance, my former husband never apologized for being unfaithful; my brother was merciless in taunting me.*)

1. _____

_____

_____

2. _____

_____

_____

What undesirable messages might be communicated to others if you seemed too willing to forgive? (*For instance, I might appear weak and shallow in my convictions; it could be interpreted as condoning something I strongly disagree with.*)

1. _____

_____

2. _____

_____

■ ■ ▪ ▫

Let's determine who benefits most from the choice to forgive. Certainly the person being forgiven might feel a sense of relief and perhaps would decide to mend his or her erroneous ways. However, there is no guarantee this will always occur, but we are still potentially assisting others in their spiritual growth when we choose to forgive. In Mike's situation, this potential was unfulfilled, although his parents might make changes if he chooses to manage his anger in a right way.

More importantly, Mike stood to gain by choosing forgiveness. Dr. Minirth explained, "Keep in mind that you are not obligated to forgive merely as an act of duty. It is a choice, and to have any impact on your life it needs to come from a mind of free will. So I want you to think about why you might decide to forgive. I hope you will learn that it has positive consequences for you. One of them is that you'll be more attuned to godly traits."

"I know you're right," Mike replied. "I guess I'll have to remind myself that God wants me to forgive because of the positive impact it will have on my life."

"God never asks you to do something harmful to yourself. When He instructs you to forgive, it is because He loves you enough to guide you in the way of holiness. A clean slate with God can become your motive for forgiveness."

■ ■ ■ ■

What positive rewards could you expect when you choose to forgive people who do not really deserve it? *(For instance, I'd be a lot less obsessed with their mistreatment of me, and that would put me in a better mood with my family.)*

1. _____

_____

2. _____

_____

■ ■ ■ ■

An even higher motive to forgive lies in the fact that it pleases God when we yield to His guidance. Forgiveness honors Him. Through this choice we can communicate to Him, *I am not inclined to choose forgiveness, but I so respect Your truth that I will yield to Your ways.* Forgiveness is an act of humility.

> ### Forgiveness is an act of humility.

Do you envision God as a stern taskmaster who insists that you follow His rules regarding forgiveness? If so, it will be difficult to relinquish your anger; most of us resist forced change. Do you, however, think of

God as a dear parent who delights in your willingness to rest in Him? If so, forgiveness will not be a drudgery, but a relief. How our burdens are lightened when we realize that when humans fail us, we can find reinforcement in a God who respects our submission to Him!

Check the following statements you can agree with.

☐ Vengeance or retribution is not mine, but God's.

☐ Forgiveness allows me to detach myself from another person's inappropriateness. It gives me freedom.

☐ Forgiveness pleases God because it allows Him to fill me with His character.

☐ An unwillingness to forgive only creates imprisonment. I become like the one who has disrespected me.

☐ I can choose to hold a grudge if I really want to; forgiveness is not obligatory.

☐ My other relationships are enhanced greatly when I am willing to forgive.

Why should I try when no one else does?

In one of his early discussions with Dr. Minirth, Mike said, "You know the most frustrating aspect of my counseling? My dad ought to be the one sitting in this chair. He's the one with the major-league problems. Anything you see wrong in me is due to his fathering."

"Has he ever shown any inclination to seek counseling or at least to talk over his problems with you?"

"Are you kidding? He'd rather die first! That's what makes everything so unfair. Why should I be the one struggling when he's going to continue his life in the same old way?"

Mike's question was quite normal, although it was also very idealistic. Anger reduction is much easier when everyone involved makes equal effort toward harmony. But that's not likely in many cases. Note some common examples of unfair circumstances in which one person lags behind the efforts of another to restore the relationship:

A mother is very conscientious about efforts to correct communication problems with her strong-willed son. But her anger increases each time she is reminded of her husband's cavalier attitude toward family problems.

A hardworking employee senses he is the only one who consistently shows courtesy in the office. He is tempted to "join the crowd" by being just as cynical toward the job as the rest of the workers.

A grown man tries to make amends with his brother for an old feud, but the brother refuses to answer letters or receive phone calls.

All of these people could justifiably shout, "It's not fair!" They could cling to their anger, feeling superior in the knowledge that they had not succumbed to the petty ways of another. But what would it gain them?

■ ■ ■ ■

Have you ever been willing to make amends, only to be rebuffed? (For instance, my husband still won't talk to me about our long-standing financial problems.)

1. _____

_____

2. _____

_____

What cynical thoughts do you nurse when you perceive that you are being treated unfairly? (For instance, I want to scold that person for being so obstinate.)

1. _____

_____

2. _____

_____

■ ■ ■ ■

When we require fairness as a prerequisite for anger management, we ask for trouble. In ancient Corinth, an angry dispute festered for a long time because fairness could not be reached. The issue was meat that had been offered in pagan animal sacrifices but eventually sold in the open market to Christians who were discount shopping. In anger, Christians condemned one another for opposing points of view. The rift would not go away. "It's not fair!" each group would claim, justifying their anger because of the obstinacy of the other.

Can you relate? Perhaps you've got a very strong opinion about right and wrong, but the person you'd like to change won't give you the time of day. You want to resolve the problem, but in light of the other person's stubborn ignorance you stay stuck in your anger, waiting for him or her to make the right move.

Mike explained it this way: "You might think my parents could be mature enough to just hear my point of view. But they won't. So if they are so stubborn in their self-serving rationalizations I shouldn't be expected to play the hero role and just smile and make everything all right."

Mike's problem was one of dependency. He was allowing his emotional composure to be so closely linked to his parents' response that he had lost any sense of personal initiative.

The apostle Paul addressed this very problem when he wrote to the Corinthians about their anger over the meat-eating issue. First he told them, "Knowledge puffs up, but love edifies" (1 Corinthians 8:1). In other words, "You can feel so correct about your opinions that your knowledge becomes your own worst enemy. You've lost your ability to live in love, because you are 'correctly' clinging to your anger." Paul then identified the group that believed it was permissible to eat the meat as the winners of the argument. Their knowledge indeed was superior. But in a strange twist he turned right around and said, in effect, "Forget for the moment how correct you are and release your anger. Show some leadership by doing what is loving rather than insisting on fairness."

> Knowledge puffs up, but love edifies.
> —1 Corinthians 8:1

Dr. Minirth explained to Mike, "I've got to compliment you on the fact that in spite of shortcomings in your past, you possess a wisdom that can serve you well. But with your wisdom comes a price. You will often be the only one who knows how to resolve angry conflicts. So, rather than using your maturity to prove to others how they must change, you may be required to take the lead in healing wounds."

"Even if it means letting my parents continue to be blind to their misdeeds?"

"I'm afraid that may be the case, Mike. You could make the most eloquent arguments to them about resolving your conflicts, but to no avail. So don't get hung up on what they do. Your job is to maintain the highest level of stability in yourself. Be thankful you can have an emotionally healthy life independent of their entrenched ways."

■ ■ ■ ▪

If you chose to let go of your anger in spite of another's impropriety, what advantages would you find? *(For instance, I'd feel an inner satisfaction, knowing my life could be steady even though others may choose to dislike me.)*

1. _____

   _____

2. _____

   _____

■ ■ ■ ▪

Anger Is a Familiar Habit

Dr. Minirth had been quite direct with Mike, and it was producing positive results. His message could be summarized, "You have historical justifications for feeling angry, but ultimately your emotional stability will be anchored in your own determination."

One day Mike grinned as he asked the doctor, "Don't you get

frustrated with stubborn guys like me who seem bent on staying angry in spite of all your efforts to guide us to a new way of living?"

"As a matter of fact, it *can* feel exasperating when I discover that some people seem to enjoy staying angry. You might even refer to some of these people as anger addicts. Inwardly, something tells them that their anger is harmful, yet it is such a familiar habit they wouldn't know how to live without it."

Just as we can get hooked on alcohol or food or materialism, we can become hooked on anger. We can go back to it again and again, not because we particularly like the anger but because it is such a familiar part of our routine. We can hardly imagine responding to tension any other way. When this happens, we say the subconscious mind is at work. Choices are made, but they are made so automatically we do not take the time to consciously acknowledge what we are selecting.

To determine if you lean toward addictive anger tendencies, check the following items that apply to you.

☐ Sometimes my angry response far exceeds the importance of the conflict at hand.

☐ Too many of my arguments at home seem to be a repeat of earlier disagreements.

☐ I can nurse grudges even when the reason for feeling angry is illogical.

☐ At times I experience a "free-floating" anger, a strong emotion that is not tied to any particular event.

☐ Inwardly I direct myself to stop my angry behavior, but it continues in spite of my self-instructions.

☐ I respond to my world with an easy cynicism or skepticism.

☐ I can experience rapid mood changes; one moment I'm fine, then suddenly I become perturbed.

☐ Others have told me they're never quite sure how I will respond to a sensitive topic.

☐ I have a history of broken relationships or of few close relationships.

☐ Somehow I don't seem to learn from past mistakes as well as I should.

If you checked at least five of these statements, you are probably holding on to your anger because it has become a habit. Whether or not you are consciously aware of it, anger has become a core element in your identity.

In the previous chapters we have examined several factors underlying an angry disposition. Adjustments in thought and in lifestyle have been offered to counter this anger. It is possible to reduce your tendency toward anger through insight and determination. But before that happens, you must ask yourself, *Am I ready for a new manner of life, perhaps even a new identity?*

Dr. Minirth put a question to Mike: "Try to imagine what you would be like if you chose to develop alternatives to your familiar angry responses. How would you be different?"

"Wow, that's a good question! My wife wouldn't know what got into me. I'm not sure what I'd be like."

"Think hard. You've said many times you'd like to be less angry. What would you like to be instead?"

"Well, for starters, I guess I'd like to be more accommodating of differences. I'd be less touchy, more accepting. I'd try to be more encouraging, I guess, instead of my usual critical self. You know, I hate to admit it, but I've become so accustomed to being angry that I don't think much about what you are asking of me."

■ ■ ■ ■

If you could set aside your habitual anger, what healthy traits would you choose instead? *(For instance, I'd develop more of a reputation for listening to others.)*

1. _____

   _____

2. _____

   _____

3. _____

   _____

4. _____

   _____

■ ■ ■ ■ ■

Throughout this book, this underlying theme has guided our examination of anger: No matter what your background or current circumstances, you have a *choice* in the direction of your emotions. While you cannot dictate which emotions will or will not enter your mind, you have a lot to say about the intensity of that emotion. You can choose to set aside nonproductive expressions of anger, such as criticism or pouting, in favor of healthier expressions, such as calm firmness or decisiveness.

Dr. Minirth explained to Mike, "In secular psychology the term *determinism* implies that your personal pluses and minuses are a direct by-product of your past. But our Christian view does not endorse determinism entirely. While your emotions are indeed influenced by your background, you still have a responsibility before God to decide if you will let Him guide your emotions. At some point you become personally accountable for your own choices."

"So that's why you've leaned on me to focus less on my parents' behavior and more on my own choices," said Mike. "You're telling me if I stay angry it's because I'm choosing to remain with something familiar rather than venturing into a newer, less familiar way of life."

"That's right. And I hope you can hear the spirit in which I am saying this. Rather than being insensitive to your past sufferings, I want to offer hope. You *can* start anew. That's a central message of the Christian faith."

■ ■ ■ ■

Respond to the following sentences.

I will take increased responsibility for my anger by letting go of my tendency to _____

_____

_____

Although others have wronged me, I will choose to _____

_____

_____

Instead of focusing on my right to feel angry, I will focus on _____

_____

_____

13

:: Being Accountable

■ Step 13. Be accountable for your ongoing growth and open about your anger management.

Tom, the embittered single father mentioned in Chapter 1, had continued with counseling for several months. He and Dr. Carter discussed numerous concepts related to his anger, and by understanding himself more clearly he had become less susceptible to his passive-aggressive patterns. In one of their final sessions he said, "I've discovered that I hide anger behind my nice-guy reputation, but that only postpones the misery caused by the emotion. It's been very refreshing to learn that I can communicate my feelings without worrying I will somehow be rejected. In fact, when I keep my emotional slate clean, my relationships are more rewarding."

"Out of curiosity, Tom, what adjustments have you made that indicate a true change of direction in your anger management?" Dr. Carter asked.

"Probably my most telling adjustment is that I don't pout any more. I used to get really agitated at my former wife because of her rejection, but I'd never tell anyone how I felt. I'd just withdraw and sulk. And you can imagine how it affected my overall disposition. I was less approachable, more moody and cynical."

"But you've given up pouting? What have you put in its place?"

"I've decided to be more honest about how I feel and more immediate in expressing those feelings. I've learned that if I try to hide my anger, it will be expressed any way in behavior like cynicism, criticism, grouchiness, and the like. But by being open and properly assertive I can keep my anger from being so distasteful."

Tom had come full circle in his anger management efforts. In general, there were three elements to his turnaround: (1) identifying the anger in its many forms, (2) understanding the factors causing him to stay angry (this would include acknowledging such issues as his pride, inferiority struggles, control needs, and dependencies), and (3) yielding his mind to a healthy lifestyle consistent with Scripture.

Dr. Carter told him, "You could have succeeded in the first two steps, but if you had failed to implement the third step, your efforts would have been wasted. New insights and awareness mean little until they prompt you to make significant adjustments in your lifestyle."

APPLYING YOUR INSIGHTS

To promote a more rewarding and responsible manner of relating, the causes of your anger must be identified. An awakened mind should result in changed patterns of living. You can make several adjustments in your behavior to confirm that you have succeeded in managing your anger: (1) set goals to become more relational, (2) make amends, (3) choose to be positive in your communication, and finally, (4) be authentic. Let's look at each of these adjustments more closely.

Set Goals to Become More Relational

Persistent anger inhibits success in relationships because an angry person repels others. We noted in Chapter 1 that most anger is linked to the preservation of worth, needs, and convictions. As legitimate as that purpose can be, when anger is expressed improperly it not only fails to achieve its goal, it hinders us from connecting effectively with others. Misused anger creates an emotional atmosphere of rejection, pessimism, or self-centeredness, ultimately leaving everyone involved dissatisfied.

When anger is properly asserted or responsibly dropped, the increased camaraderie and harmony are possible and many desirable qualities can surface.

Tom told Dr. Carter, "My greatest joy is spending time with my son and daughter. They are almost fully grown now, so our conversations can be very meaningful. But when I was in my disgruntled mode, we lost the ability to enjoy each other's company. I didn't consciously intend to repel them, but that's what happened too often."

> When anger is expressed improperly it not only fails to achieve its goal, it hinders us from connecting effectively with others.

"You're saying your new understanding of yourself has propelled you toward new successes in your relationships. What's different at this point?"

"Several things. My anger kept me focused on myself. But now I make a concerted effort to be tuned in to my kids' world. I genuinely want to know about their lives. I'm a better listener. My conversations are livelier. I'm more patient and accepting when we're on different wavelengths. I laugh easily."

"I'm really encouraged for you, Tom. You're experiencing genuine joy!" said Dr. Carter.

■ ■ ■ ■

As you find balance in your anger, what relationship goals will become more prominent? (For instance, I'll be genuinely concerned about my spouse's needs; I'll carry on a conversation without eventually turning attention toward my woes.)

1. _____

_____

_____

2. _____

_____

_____

3. _____

_____

_____

■ ■ ■ ▪

Check the following statements you can truly agree with.

☐ I want to be known as someone who finds the good in others.

☐ I can find joy in small places, such as a quiet dinner with family members or spending a day outdoors with neighbors.

☐ Doing good is a delight, not a duty.

☐ Patience does not have to be forced. I can be patient because I am at peace with myself.

☐ I've decided to remain respectful even when the person in front of me is not respectful.

☐ Not only do I not mind hearing others' problems, I want to be known as one who is approachable.

☐ Even when problems are not completely resolved, I can be courteous.

☐ It is only fair that I accept others' imperfections, just as I want them to accept mine.

☐ I won't become uptight when my day becomes hectic; life's too short to remain chronically anxious.

In our counseling practices we have known many people who have achieved the look of success but who are actually miserable because of untamed anger. Ultimately, they are not successful at all. The highest aim in living is to know how to connect voluntarily with others in God's love.

Make Amends with Those You Have Wronged

An inevitable by-product of misguided anger is damaged relationships. Families have collapsed because of unresolved anger. Business partnerships, friendships, and church fellowships have suffered because people cling too powerfully to their anger. By the time people decide to remedy this emotion they can probably point to several significant relationships that have been devastated, or at least hindered.

It is not enough for us to resolve to move forward with a new perspective on managing anger. To truly find balance we must be willing to make amends with those who have been hurt by our past behavior and attitudes. This can come in different forms:

> To truly find balance we must be willing to make amends with those who have been hurt by our past behavior and attitudes.

- You can ask an offended family member or friend to forgive you for specific wrongs.

- You can explain to that person how you will change your manner of communicating.

- You can do favors or perform corrective deeds to show you are not just giving lip service to your changed attitudes.

- You can openly explain to anyone who needs to know how you will go forward with a different way of life.

■ ■ ■ ■

As you show a new attitude regarding your anger, what specific amends can you make that could promote healing? (*For instance, I can tell my brother he will no longer have to worry that I will criticize him to other family members; I can ask my coworker to forgive me for being so inattentive.*)

1. _____

_____

_____

2. _____

_____

_____

3. _____

   _____

   _____

■ ■ ■ ■

Tom told Dr. Carter, "My former wife and I don't have much communication anymore. But we do have to talk about plans with finances and the kids. She's hurt by my anger because I've been stubborn and obstinate many times. I want to change, but I'm not sure she will believe me if I just ask her to forgive me."

"It is not your primary task to convince her of your changed way of life," said Dr. Carter. "Let her come to terms about the anger she holds toward you. But you can make a start in a new relationship with her by confessing your wrong modes of anger and asking her forgiveness."

"She'd be stunned to hear me say, 'I was wrong.' But I'm up to it. What should I do, though, if she chooses not to forgive me?"

"Don't make your progress dependent on her reaction. Once you determine to relate differently with her, decide what changes would be in order, then proceed. Can you think of the adjustments you would make?"

"First, I wouldn't procrastinate when she needs me to respond to a decision about the kids. I've done that in the past, knowing it would drive her crazy. Second, I wouldn't enter into guilt-inducing arguments with her. I'd be more calm in stating my feelings, and then I would respect her differentness. Finally, I could just maintain a more pleasant overall demeanor. I don't have to appear disgruntled every time I speak with her. I need to get beyond the anger hiding behind my hurt."

"That's a pretty tall order. Those adjustments are easier said than done," Dr. Carter said.

"But Dr. Carter, I'm going to make the changes because I'm tired of being angry. Making peace with my former wife is the best thing that could happen to me."

■ ■ ■ ■

How about you? What adjustments do you need to make as part of your commitment to change? (*For instance, I'd tell my sister I was wrong*

in the way I spoke condescendingly and would vow to be more sensitive;
I'd ask my dad if we could put past tensions behind and relate as adults.)

1. _____
_____
_____

2. _____
_____
_____

3. _____
_____
_____

■ ■ ■ ■

Some angry people would like to make amends, but they find it impossible to do so directly because of the other person's unavailability. For example, an adult child of abuse may want to settle an angry issue with a parent who has died. Or you may try to make amends with a former friend who refuses to return your phone calls. What can be done?

First, have a healing heart, even if the communication cannot go full circle. Know inwardly that you truly desire to bear no grudges. Then write out your feelings and plans. This can be done in a journal or perhaps an unmailed letter. By writing, you can see your needs in black and white; this can make them seem less theoretical and more tangible.

As you write, be honest about the hurt and pain you have felt. Describe the anguish you have experienced. Share how you have arrived at the decision to forgive. Then make statements that reflect your forgiving spirit.

After writing several letters to his father, detailing past events of anger, one man explained to Dr. Minirth, "By putting my feelings on paper, I was able to see inside myself as I never had before. I realized that my anger was legitimate, but I also saw how it would harm me if I chose to cling to it. I've kept the letters in my desk, and when I am reminded of my past pain I pull them out and reread them. Those letters have become my personal declaration of independence."

■ ■ ■ ■

What experiences from your past involve people who are no longer available to open communication? *(For instance, My father died, and we had an ongoing grudge regarding his alcoholism.)*

1. _____

_____

_____

2. _____

_____

_____

What could you tell that person that would aid you in making amends for the past? *(For instance, I would apologize to my father for the cruel things I said about him.)*

1. _____

_____

_____

2. _____

_____

_____

■ ■ ■ ■

While there are no guarantees that we can tie down all loose ends involving past anger, we can proceed with a clean future when we are willing to take the lead in our commitments to emotional healthiness.

Choose to Be Positive in Your Communication

When you have been saddled with anger for any length of time, you will notice that your attitude leans toward pessimism. Rather than being friendly or encouraging or winsome, too often you are cynical or critical or withdrawn. Ongoing anger inhibits positive traits.

Once you understand the meaning and underlying causes of your anger, you can formulate goals that will reflect a change of heart. You can deliberately set out to establish a reputation as someone who is caring rather than full of grudges.

Check the following sentences that express your desires for a changed life.

- ☐ I'd like to develop a greater reputation as an encouraging person.

- ☐ I know I need to be less critical and more friendly with family and friends.

- ☐ Showing an enthusiasm toward others' lifestyle interests can be rewarding.

- ☐ Commenting on what is right will take priority over commenting about what is wrong.

- ☐ When I'm with others, I want to set an upbeat tone or initiate friendly exchange.

- ☐ I want to be more genuine, with no more games of phoniness or cover-up.

- ☐ Rather than brewing over minor problems, I intend to give them less attention.

- ☐ True joy and the accompanying laughter and fellowship with friends is what I want.

- ☐ I intend to be less rigid and more flexible as I interact with others.

- ☐ I'll be a better listener since I won't be so consumed with myself.

Ephesians 4:31 tells us to put away "all bitterness, wrath, anger, clamor, and evil speaking," along with all malice. But it does not stop at these. The next verse

> Let all bitterness, wrath, anger, clamor, and evil speaking be put away from you, with all malice.—Ephesians 4:31

instructs us to be kind, tenderhearted, and forgiving. The true test of anger management lies in who you become after you have chosen to manage your anger differently.

■ ■ ■ ■ ▫

What adjustments do you need to make to show you are less pessimistic and more relational? *(For instance, each night I could remember to compliment my children for what I like about them, rather than just scolding them for what I don't like.)*

1. _____

   _____

   _____

2. _____

   _____

   _____

3. _____

   _____

   _____

■ ■ ■ ▫

As Tom and Dr. Carter summarized his sessions, they discussed how his awakened mind could lead him toward more fruitful relationships. "I hate to admit it," said Tom, "but for a couple of years I was so captivated by my simmering anger that I didn't even think about being tuned in to others' needs. I knew I ought to be more friendly, but I just didn't care about expending the energy on it."

"I guess we could say you spent so much of your emotional energy on being irritated you used it all up. Being tuned in to others requires effort," noted Dr. Carter.

"It does, but it's a very rewarding effort. As I think about the anger I felt about my divorce, I realize how unavailable I was to my son and daughter."

"So what's different now that you're more aware of your emotions?"

"Mainly, I'm determined to show my kids what good family relating can be like. I enjoy the prospect of talking maturely with them about their philosophies of living. Scott's in high school and the girls flock around him. So we talk freely about how to show respect to a woman and how not to get bogged down in trivial worries. It's neat to share things like that with my son!"

Dr. Carter smiled. "I'll bet you never had discussions like that with your dad when you were his age. It's got to be rewarding to know that because of your pain you are better equipped to launch him into adulthood with an awareness of who he is."

■ ■ ■ ■

Respond to the following sentences:

When I am caught in anger, my primary goal seems to be _____

_____

As I choose to moderate my anger, my new goal will be to _____

_____

■ ■ ■ ■

Be Authentic about Your Anger Management Efforts

"Tom, I'm eager to see that your anger adjustments are lasting," said Dr. Carter, "and there's one key element that will be vital. You'll need to be open about your changes with people who know you well."

"Are you suggesting I bare my soul to people about what I've been going through?"

"Yes, I am. It's one thing to decide quietly that you will handle your anger more appropriately, but you will be more powerfully motivated to maintain your adjustments when you openly describe what will be different."

"That's not going to be natural," Tom admitted. "I've never really wanted people to know I've been to counseling. I don't like exposing my weaknesses. I've got my reputation to think about. What are people going to think if I tell them I've had longstanding problems with anger?"

"I doubt that you'll be ostracized, if that's what you're worried about. Certainly, you'll need to use tact as you discuss your emotions. I'm assuming, though, that as you share your experiences you'll find others will be attracted to you rather than repelled. You'll seem more real."

No one can claim immunity from emotional trauma. Yet many people like to pretend they have no such struggles. This only increases their tendency toward stress (which spawns anger) and aggravates relational tensions.

Let's be honest with each other. When you feel angry or depressed or tense, talk about it. Be open. It's virtually impossible to hide emotions anyway. They will manifest themselves whether we want them to or not. So take the guessing game out of your relationships and allow others to see behind the mask.

■ ■ ■ ■

How natural is it for you to confess your emotional struggles? *(For instance, I don't like to admit my anger because someone might hold it against me; I can talk about everyone else's problems but my own.)*

1. _____

   _____

2. _____

   _____

■ ■ ■ ■

When you confess your anger to a trusted friend, two things can occur: (1) you are able to find help and support from someone who loves you, and (2) you feel more accountable to follow through with your plans to be emotionally appropriate in the future.

At a later date, Tom reported back to Dr. Carter. "I talked with a man at my church about the battles I've been through, and I was pleasantly surprised by his response," he said.

"How did he handle it?"

"First, he told me he had struggled to tame his own temper for years. That was news to me because he always seems so calm. Then he asked how I was going to change, so I talked with him about some of the principles we've been discussing in our sessions."

"I guess it seemed out of character for you to expose your feelings like this, but it sounds like you had a rewarding experience."

"It was out of character. But I'll admit, when we went our separate ways, I wondered why I have always been so reluctant to be open. Not only did it not hurt, it felt good!"

"It gives you greater motivation to continue when you feel accepted and encouraged, doesn't it?"

■ ■ ■ ■

What could you tell someone else about yourself that would increase your sense of accountability to change? *(For instance, I'd explain to a friend how my need for control is so closely linked to my angry outbursts; I'd tell my spouse that it's my goal to listen more carefully.)*

1. _____

_____

_____

2. _____

_____

_____

■ ■ ■ ■

Galatians 6:2 tells us to bear one another's burdens, thus fulfilling the law of Christ. And what is His law? Grace. As we share our needs and plans, we create the very atmosphere of growth and encouragement that will prompt ongoing emotional healthiness.

■ Anger Treatments Today

Therapies today for anger include a plethora of choices—behavior therapy, cognitive theory, dialectical behavior theory, system theory, attachment theory, narrative theory, psychodynamic theory, and experienced dependent plastic brain theory—just to name a few.

Current anger treatments revolve around the theological, psychological, and physiological aspects of a person. If this statement sounds familiar, it might be because it sounds similar to "spirit, soul, and body" in 1 Thessalonians 5:23, penned around 51 AD. Each aspect is discussed below.

Theology Today

Anger is a common emotion; it is mentioned often in the Bible, along with other related terms (abhor, alienated, bitter, despise, enemy, enmity, fight, fury, grudge, hate, indignation, loathe, malice, rage, scorn, strife, strive, variance, vengeance, vex, war, wrath).

Whereas psychology points more toward why someone becomes angry and what he or she can do about it, theology points more toward a person's very nature. Humans possess an old nature that is ego-centered (Genesis 4:5–8; 27:42–45; 49:5–7; 1 Samuel 20:30; 1 Kings 21:4; 2 Kings 5:11; Matthew 2:16; Luke 4:28). However, in addition to this negative emotion, there is also a righteous anger (Exodus 11:8; Leviticus 10:16–17; Nehemiah 5:6–13; Psalms 97:10; Mark 3:5). Anger does not necessarily involve sin (Ephesians 4:26), but it can be a precursor of sin or a result of sin.

How a person handles anger is more important than its source. Galatians 5:22–23 give great antidotes to anger: "But the fruit of the Spirit is love, joy, peace, longsuffering, kindness, goodness, faithfulness, gentleness, self-control. Against such there is no law."

The spiritual treatments for anger today are the same as those in yesteryear.

Psychology Today

The psychological treatments used today are not the same as those in the past. In the early twentieth century, treatments revolved around such terms as repression, denial, transference, projection, insight, subconscious, and free associations.

By the 1950s psychology was changing. "Tell me more"; "I understand"; and "self-actualize" became popular terms in Carl Rogers' client-centered therapy for dealing with anger.

By the 1980s Albert Ellis and Aaron Beck were emphasizing new cognitions for inaccurate thoughts about anger with such terms as perfectionism, personalization, magnification, emotional reasoning, and arbitrary reference. With the revival of the behavior schools of Thorndike (1894), Pavlov (1920s), Watson (1913), and Skinner (1938), the cognitive behavior therapy (CBT) of today took shape. Incidentally, it is interesting that our CBT is similar to God's theory in Genesis 4:5–6: "But He did not respect Cain and his offering. And Cain was very angry, and his countenance fell. So the Lord said to Cain, Why are you angry? And why has your countenance fallen?"

Physiology Today

Although theology has not changed, psychology has changed, and physiology has been rapidly changing in dealing with anger.

Inappropriate anger can be seen in bipolar disorder, mania, schizophrenia, unipolar depression, ADHD, substance use disorders, after head injury, and during delirium. Positron Emission Tomography (PET) is in the incipient stages of viewing these disorders. Anger has been treated on-label and off-label for the above disorders with various medications, including neuroleptics, benzodiazepines, beta-blockers, anticonvulsants, and alpha agonists, depending on the disorder being treated.

In summary, anger treatments currently being used to help a counselee who is experiencing anger include:

1. Realize anger is present. Is anger present and obvious? Is it present but hidden in passive, self-defeating behaviors? If anger is present, would thinking of better ways of coping be helpful?

2. Share: anger is a common feeling. Sharing or even crying over feelings might help. Verbalizing anger to a friend, a coach, or a counselor can help.

3. Subliminate the anger. Exercise and work are initial ways to deal with anger.

4. Gain insight into the real causes of the anger. Issues in the past might need to be dealt with in the present.

5. Learn appropriate ways to deal with the anger. Being more logical in expressing anger can help. Being more kind in the expression of your anger can help.

6. Choose against letting the anger increase. Willpower can take a more powerful position in choosing against letting anger increase.

7. Challenge inaccurate thoughts that can increase anger. Have personalization, perfectionism, emotional reasoning, an event-driven life, magnification, or selective attention been problems? How?

8. Determine what persons from your past (parents, spouse, self, or others) are the real targets of your anger and choose to forgive them.

9. Let the anger expression be fair.

10. Grow in Christ. The fruit of the Spirit (love, joy, peace, longsuffering, etc.) will help you work toward relieving anger and preventing it in the future.

∷ About the Authors

Dr. Les Carter is a nationally known expert in the field of Christian counseling. He earned his B.A. from Baylor University and his M.Ed. and Ph.D. from North Texas State University. For twenty-five years he maintained a private practice at the Minirth Clinic in Richardson, Texas, specializing in the treatment of emotional and relational disorders. For eleven years he was featured weekly on the "Minirth-Meier Clinic" national radio broadcast. He currently maintains a private practice at the Southlake Psychiatric and Counseling Center in Southlake, Texas. He is the author of twenty books, including *The Freedom from Depression Workbook, The Choosing to Forgive Workbook, The Worry Workbook,* and *The Anger Trap.*

For more information, go to www.drlescarter.com. He is also featured at www.MarriageMate.com.

*   *   *

Dr. Frank Minirth is a Diplomate of the American Board of Psychiatry and Neurology, a Diplomate of the American Board of Forensic Medicine, and Certified by the American Society of Clinical Psychopharmacology. Holding doctorate degrees in both medicine and theology, he has been in private practice in the Dallas area since 1975. He is president of the Minirth Clinic, P.A., in Richardson, Texas and a consultant to the Minirth Christian Program in Harriet, Arkansas.

Dr. Minirth has authored or coauthored over one hundred books, many of which have been translated into foreign languages. His bestselling books include *Happiness Is A Choice, Love Is A Choice,* and *Love Hunger.* He has over five million books in print. He and his wife of over forty years, Mary Alice, have five daughters and two granddaughters.

For more information on the Minirth Clinic please call 1-888-646-4784, or visit www.minirthclinic.com.